Ray Hicks and the Jack Tales

Ray Hicks and the Jack Tales

✦

A Study of Appalachian History, Culture, and Philosophy

Christine Pavesic, Ph.D.

iUniverse, Inc.
New York Lincoln Shanghai

Ray Hicks and the Jack Tales
A Study of Appalachian History, Culture, and Philosophy

Copyright © 2005 by Christine L. Pavesic

All rights reserved. No part of this book may be used or reproduced by any means, graphic, electronic, or mechanical, including photocopying, recording, taping or by any information storage retrieval system without the written permission of the publisher except in the case of brief quotations embodied in critical articles and reviews.

iUniverse books may be ordered through booksellers or by contacting:

iUniverse
2021 Pine Lake Road, Suite 100
Lincoln, NE 68512
www.iuniverse.com
1-800-Authors (1-800-288-4677)

ISBN-13: 978-0-595-36377-3 (pbk)
ISBN-13: 978-0-595-80814-4 (ebk)
ISBN-10: 0-595-36377-6 (pbk)
ISBN-10: 0-595-80814-X (ebk)

Printed in the United States of America

To Dad

Contents

Preface xi

CHAPTER 1   The Origins of the Jack Tale Tradition 1

CHAPTER 2   The Storyteller From Beech Mountain: Ray Hicks
And Traditional Appalachian Jack Tales 16

- *Jack Represents a Community* *17*
- *The Storyteller Becomes His Character.* *26*

CHAPTER 3   The Form of Oral Storytelling. 34

- *The Elements of Stories.* *34*
- *Morphology of Folktales* *39*
- *Oral Art Form in a Literate Society.* *44*
- *Oral Composition* *45*
- *Composition in Performance.* *48*
- *Performance Craft.* *52*

CHAPTER 4   Passing the Torch: Ray Hicks's Influence on the
Storytellers From Beech Mountain and Beyond. 56

- *Hicks's Influence on Beech Mountain Storytellers* *59*
- *Hicks's Influence Beyond Beech Mountain.* *69*

Conclusion 75

Works Cited 83

About the Author 89

Endnotes. 91

Acknowledgements

The author would like to express sincere gratitude to Dr. James Giles for all of his help and encouragement, to Jim May for all of his efforts to keep storytelling alive and flourishing, and, especially, to Ray Hicks for his inspirational life and work.

Preface

There comes an old man and his three sons...I could match this beginning with an old tale.

—William Shakespeare

Mankind has always told stories, whether simple, anecdotal tales about everyday experiences or fantastic tales spun from the limitless source of human imagination. Each story begins with a moment, an experience, or a feeling that defines its nature. In *Old Tales and New Truths*, James Roy King suggests that these narratives summon both the teller and the audience to forgotten or neglected possibilities or experiences that have the potential to assume life-enhancing or transcendental implications (2). Whether from an ancient or a highly mechanized society, stories have been told for the same reasons: to educate, to entertain, to explain, to honor the past, and to record the experience of human existence. In every culture there is evidence of storytelling, by people relieving the monotony of their everyday lives at home and at work collecting the harvest, weaving, or performing everyday tasks and by the professional minstrels, gleemen, and scops who guard the history of a people. Like other forms of literature, folk tales and stories have always had a place of special importance in broadening experience, alerting listeners in highly personal ways to other arrangements and interpretations of experience. Every person has a story to tell that helps to define the traditions, values, rites of passage, ceremonies, and legends that are a part of life.

In the twenty-first century, human beings still enjoy stories, for our lives remain bound irrevocably by narrative. Tales that may outwardly seem ordinary are able to catch listeners up in a complex spell and help them make sense of the world. In this study, I shall explore both the oral and written development of contemporary American storytelling and trends in society that have led to its current popularity and literary significance. The study centers on folktales in the Appalachian oral traditions and examines both the history and the cultural impact of them. In it I will initially survey existing scholarship concerning orality and the European origins of the Jack Tales and then focus upon a prominent Appalachian recorder of the tales, Ray Hicks, and his influence upon other storytellers.

First, I will analyze the history of The Jack Tales from the first published version in the fifteenth century down to modern-day narratives. The Jack Tales are stories of ancient origin, are stories that have an unbroken chain of transmission, and are stories that not only have been preserved through the centuries, but altered and enhanced by the passage of time. The tales exist at the forefront of Indo-European oral tradition and most countries boast of their own additions to the tradition. Examining both the tales and the reasons behind their enduring presence is crucial to understanding the nature of "Jack's" cultural presence.

Second, I will undertake my own analysis of the storytelling methods of Ray Hicks and his special influence on the Jack Tales. Being involved in the oral arts (and with the Jack Tales in particular) has not only shaped Hicks's life, but has allowed him to have an impact upon the lives of other Appalachian natives.

Third, I will explore the basic elements of the oral tradition and show how American storytellers have preserved the techniques of oral composition, composition in performance, and performance craft within a literate culture. Because contemporary American storytellers, unlike those in preliterate times, take their art from two distinct traditions, one oral, the other written, it is important both to clarify the conflicts between oral works and printed works and to understand the effects they have upon one another.

Finally, I will attempt to demonstrate how Hicks's popularity as a storyteller has influenced members of subsequent generations to move beyond the general confines of their own lives and access the historical, philosophical, religious, and regional knowledge of the Beech Mountain culture.

For centuries the art of oral storytelling has flourished. Oral narratives exist in every culture. Many people search for any type of opening to begin a tale. Stories spontaneously spring from something as simple as seeing an old man and his three sons walking down a road. Storytellers not only work from these openings to develop tales that truly meet the moment and arouse a sense of recognition in their listeners, they take something real (the old man and his three sons) and create an image in their fictional world. This immersion into a fictional construction alters the image, so those who have listened to the tale will be more likely to recall the narrative when confronted by the image in real life. The listeners will then be able to switch roles and generate their own variations of the original tale and continue the storytelling cycle.

1

The Origins of the Jack Tale Tradition

"Our own language affords many [stories] of excellent use and instruction, finely calculated to sow the seeds of virtue in youth…Such is the history of John the Great, who, by his brave and heroic actions against men of large and athletic bodies, obtained the glorious appellation of the Giant-killer."

—Henry Fielding

In an interview recorded at Berea College, Kentucky, Richard Chase describes his first encounter with the Jack Tales. Chase met Marshall Ward at a meeting in Raleigh, North Carolina, that had been organized for Emergency Relief in Education. Ward explained to Chase that his family had a tradition of storytelling "handed down from generation to generation" (Chase 11). This was Chase's first exposure to the existence of the Jack Tales and he was excited at the prospect of uncovering an active tale-telling tradition in the Appalachian mountain area.

Since the publication of Chase's *Jack Tales* in 1943, the character of Jack and the stories he inspired have received more attention and aroused more critical discourse than any other oral art form from the Appalachians. The Jack Tales are stories of ancient origin; are stories that have an unbroken chain of transmission; and are stories that have not only been preserved throughout the centuries, but altered and enhanced by the passage of time. One wishes to discover the origins of such tales, to understand why they continue to be told, and to observe the changes in the nature of the Jack Tales and in the character of Jack that have taken place over the years. The important questions surrounding the tales do not simply concern the meaning of particular words within the narratives or the motives of particular "Jack" characters; they concern the fact of the Jack Tales' enduring presence and cultural dominance. In *The Jack Tales*, Chase describes Jack as representative of the American people, a characterization that is echoed by many modern-day critics (xii). In "Jacks: The Name, the Tales, the American Traditions," Carl Lindahl explains that the character of Jack reflects the self-image of America (xiv). Going one step further, Sobol describes Jack in "The Jack Tales: Coming From Afar" as "a sign in English for Everyman" (17). The question arises as to when modern American critics decided that "Jack" was the most representative portrayal of the common man? What prejudices and convictions might have influenced their decisions? On what evidence or reasoning did they justify their verdict?

These questions may appear abstract in form, but they quickly translate into simple issues of social behavior. For example, during the National Storytelling festival in Jonesborough, Tennessee, many different oral artists are invited to perform, but no living storyteller seems to have the celebrity—the intense audience appeal—as Ray Hicks, whose speciality is the Jack Tales. In an interview with Sobol for *The Storyteller's Journey*, Steve Sanfield relates his experience with Hicks:

> I heard somebody say, "Oh, we need somebody to pick up Ray Hicks…" I thought this was a great opportunity. And I got lost finding him…But he played like, "Oh, is today the day? Do we have to go today? I don't know if I want to go…" And I'm supposed to bring him back to this festival. And he's sitting around, and then he starts tellin' me stories…and it was fine with me if we never went.
>
> So we drove on to Jonesborough. And I literally pull up at the main tent. And as soon as I pull up, he's surrounded! The car is surrounded…And they literally drag him out from the car and onto the stage. It was like that. (Sobol 106-107)

Hicks' reception at the festival is remarkably similar to ones accorded to American movie actors or rock stars. One expects this type of frenzy to accompany multi-million dollar projects designed to stimulate the senses and inflame the passions. Yet Hicks's performance consists of a lone performer sitting on a stage telling stories about a boy/man named Jack. One simply has to wonder about the value placed upon the stories by the audience.

The Jack Tales cannot be separated from the values that people have placed within those works. Art is never free of its cultural and historical references—it does not spring from a void, but from needs within a culture. The storytellers reflect the dominant intellectual and political concerns of a period and the unique characteristics of a culture. Like other art forms, a Jack Tale reflects the society that creates it.

It should not be a surprise that different cultures have interpreted the Jack Tales in different ways. But how did one prevailing interpretation give way to another? When and why did people stop answering one question and start asking another? Because of their long and varied history, the Jack Tales provide some of the best specimens in English for studying such cultural development.

The North American Jack Tales first appeared in historical records in the nineteenth century. Evidence for this tradition is provided by Rev. Dr. Joseph Doddridge in his notes (published 1824) concerning frontier life in Western Pennsylvania and Virginia (now West Virginia) between 1763 and 1783. Doddridge writes:

> Dramatic narrations, chiefly concerning Jack and the Giant, furnished our young people with another source of amusement during their leisure hours. Many of those tales were lengthy, and embraced a considerable range of incident...and were so arranged as to the different incidents of the narration, that they were easily committed to memory. They certainly have been handed down from generation to generation, from time immemorial. (159)

In *A History of the Valley of Virginia* (1833), Samual Kercheval discusses his early experiences in Virginia and repeats this description of the Jack Tales. The stories mirror the chapbook tales that were popular in the English-speaking world at the time. Indeed, there is evidence to suggest that immigrants from England, Scotland, and Ireland brought their Jack Tales with them to the new country. The history of the American Jack Tales thus begins in the "old world" with tales that encompass a vast tradition.

The first recorded version in English of a Jack Tale, "Jack and His Step-Dame," was published in England during the fifteenth century. It is a two-part poem which also includes "The Friar and the Boy." In Britain both segments of the poem gained great popularity and were frequently reprinted throughout the sixteenth and seventeenth centuries. In the eighteenth century the two parts of the poem were often bound together in chapbooks.

The complete version of "Jack and His Step-Dame" presents Jack as a youth who is abused by his stepmother. After sharing his food with a beggar, Jack proves his worth. He is granted three wishes which include a bow and arrows that never miss their mark, a magical pipe that compels all listeners to dance, and a spell that makes the step-dame pass wind explosively whenever she looks with anger upon Jack:

> Then she stared in his [Jack's] face

4   Ray Hicks and the Jack Tales

> And anon she let go a blaste
> That she mad hem all agaste
> That wer within pat place
> All they lowgh and had good game.
> The wyffe wex red for shame (Furrow 109-110).

By utilizing the three wishes, Jack is able to punish his stepmother and the wicked Friar who comes to her aid and tries to have Jack executed.

"Jack and His Step-Dame" is an excellent example of the scatological sides of the Jack Tales. This type of traditional oral narrative with its satirical nature, vigor, crude humor, and ridicule of conventional morality can be viewed as following the same form as the fabliau[1]—a poetry form utilized by Chaucer, Boccaccio, and La Fontaine. Within both the Jack Tales and the fablieux, priests and monks are portrayed as lechers, merchant's wives are easily and frequently seduced, and clever young men perpetually make fools of sober and stuffy elders.

By the nineteenth century in England, new advances in technology affected the way the Jack Tales were presented to the public. As Richard D. Altick reveals in *Victorian People and Ideas*, the social processes that shaped Victorian thought are depicted in the manufacture and sale of printed matter, an industry essential in helping to form the public perception of the traditional stories and folktales. Mechanical innovations revolutionized productivity, efficiency, prices, and working conditions in the printing industry. In the 1800s all paper was made by hand from rags; by 1900, one hundred times as much paper was being manufactured by machine at prices averaging one-tenth of those prevailing a century before. The machine presses developed for book production could work eight times faster than the manually operated presses they replaced. This reduced the price of books to the point where most people could afford to purchase their own works of literature and no longer had to depend upon lending libraries (64-66).

With the advances in technology making more books available, Altick reveals, the national literacy rates for adults in the Victorian era had risen from sixty-seven percent (male) and fifty-one percent (female) in 1841 to almost ninety-seven percent for both sexes in 1900. The literacy rates are based on the ability to sign the marriage register and do not distinguish between the social classes. The upper class probably maintained the same level of literacy as prior centuries and the working class did not have living conditions conducive to the reading habit, so the vast increase of "readers" had to come from the middle class (Altick 59-62).

The majority of the works produced were targeted for the levels of society which were literate and able to afford a purchase. In order to garner the most sales, the publishers changed their products. For example, upper and middle class Victorian readers wanted the Jack Tales to be charming, to reflect the gender roles of the time, and above all to instruct children in appropriate morality. Publishers sanitized the tales by toning down the violence and simplifying the narratives.

Many of the folktales published during the Victorian era were intended for children. Victorians romanticized the idea of childhood as something quite separate from adult life. Children were considered inherently innocent and in need of protection from the burdens of adulthood[2]—a theme that runs through many Victorian works, such as Lewis Carroll's Alice books and J.M. Barrie's *Peter Pan*.

There was money to be made by exploiting the Victorian love affair with childhood; publishers had found a market, and they needed a product with which to fill it. Cheap story material was available to the publishers by taking stories from the vast English oral tradition, simplifying the tales for young readers, and further revising the stories to conform to Victorian gender roles and moral standards.

By 1823, Opie and Opie explain in *The Classic Fairy Tales*, the sale of books in England written from oral traditional tales had been invigorated by the publication of *German Popular Stories*, which had been translated by Edgar Taylor from the *Kinder-und Haus Märchen* of Jacob and William Grimm. The Grimms' tales were encoded with tributes to thrift, honesty, patience, obedience, and other noble civic virtues: they endorsed contemporary ethical values and social norms. The folktales obviously struck a chord with the British public and, by 1870, had been incorporated into the teaching curriculum of many schools (23).

"Jack and His Step-Dame" underwent several changes in the Grimms' version, "The Jew in the Thornbush," although the main features of the story remain the same: Jack befriends a beggar and is granted three wishes. To mirror the technological advances occurring in the culture, the bow and arrows that will not miss their mark are upgraded to a gun that will never miss its target. The pipe that compels all listeners to dance becomes a violin with the same attributes. Since they are writing for children, however, the Grimm brothers institute a major change with the final wish—instead of a spell that makes the step-dame pass wind explosively, Jack is given a spell which insures his every request is granted.

While the Grimms retain the basic form of the oral tradition, the sexuality and bawdy humor of the tale all but disappear. Just as the Jewish character replaces the step-dame in the narrative, anti-Semitism substitutes for the numerous misadventures of male/female interaction. As Opie and Opie note, in the Middle Ages the prevalence of stepmothers is accounted for by the high mortality rate of

6 Ray Hicks and the Jack Tales

women during childbirth and by the practice of the surviving partner marrying again without needless delay. Girls were often forced to marry early as well (19). Thus the person raising the child and responsible for his or her welfare may be two or three times removed from the original parent. A step-mother could indeed be almost the same age as her adopted children. This familial situation is fraught with the potential for uneasiness at the least and could give rise to the emotions of anger, jealousy, resentment, and alienation—many of which are echoed in the stories of the day.

By the nineteenth century one type of social "outsider" is replaced by another. The very title, "The Jew in the Thorn Bush," creates a culturally charged expectation. As Altick observes, a person's social standing in the Victorian era is determined by his religion (31). The antipathy to the Jewish character in the story is a cultural construct—the outcome of a set of contingent circumstances surrounding trade, mercantilism, money, and usury in which the Semitic character is assumed to be enmeshed. "Too close contact with money contaminate[s] one," Altick explains, and makes a man and his family socially suspect (32). The Jewish character in the story labors under a double social handicap by being a member of a non-Anglican church and earning an income without the benefit of an intermediary.

In "Jack and His Step-Dame," Jack magically punishes his step-dame when she looks upon him with anger. She is chastised and humiliated only when her actions demonstrate a lack of maternal concern for the boy. In "The Jew in the Thorn Bush," the Jewish character is attacked without provocation. After baiting him with the term "lousy swindler," Jack forces the Semitic character to dance among the thorns:

> But the thorns ripped the Jew's coat to shreds, combed his goatee, and scratched his entire body.
> "My!" exclaimed the Jew. "What's the sense of all this fiddling? Please stop all this fiddling, sir. I have no desire to
> dance."
> [Jack] kept playing nevertheless, for he thought, You've skinned plenty of people, so now the thorns will give you some of your own treatment in return. He continued fiddling so the Jew had to leap higher and higher, and parts of his coat remained hanging on the thorns. (Grimm and Grimm 400)

The Brothers Grimm have created a major shift in the paradigms that define the abuser/victim relationship in the story. The shift amounts to a fundamental revision of the traditional roles; Jack (the apparent victim) attacks the Semitic character (the apparent abuser) before he has provocation. This situation allows the victim to have more power than the abuser. This action directly refers to culturally specific knowledge (first in Germany, and then later in England) that all "Jews" are "lousy swindlers" who deserve to dance among the thorns. The justification for Jack's actions is built upon the attitudes and icons that are accepted by the Victorians in terms of their own backgrounds, frames of reference, and social norms rather than any unscrupulous activity by the Jewish character toward Jack.

As Jack Zipes notes in "Once There Were Two Brothers Named Grimm," by the beginning of the twentieth century the Grimms' tales had enjoyed an immense popularity in the English-speaking world and had been second only to the Bible as a best-seller in many western countries. This popularity had brought about a great deal of critical attention, and advocates of various schools of thought tried to interpret and analyze the motifs of the tales. Educators and parents, however, were not so much interested in the motifs as they were in the morals and types of role models in the tales (xxix). Zipes writes that "most of the great pedagogical debates center around the brutality and cruelty in some tales, and the tendency among publishers and adapters of the tales has been to eliminate the harsh scenes" (xxix-xxx). As the Brothers Grimm had removed from the traditional stories anything of a sexual or a scatological nature, editors in the twentieth century have worked to neutralize the violent, the racist, and the sexist notions in the tales—in effect trying to create a new type of family fare, consisting of "politically correct" stories which would hold no culturally offensive content. Sanitizing the written versions of the Jack Tales to a politically correct status is just one way in which a culture can manipulate the stories. The result has been a wealth of new material to scrutinize along with the older, more familiar tales.

In twentieth-century America, the Jack Tales had a vital relationship with literature. Because of the Grimms' monetary success, other publishers attempted to sell "Jack" exclusively to children. Chase, for example, modified his language in *The Jack Tales*. In his "Preface," he admits "in editing these stories we have taken the advice of our informants, and the publisher, and retold them, in part, for this business of getting them into print" (Chase xi). But the modifications did not reach all of the storytellers who were keeping the oral tradition alive. "That's not the way they told it," Hicks asserts in an interview with Sobol for "Jack in the Raw." "He [Chase] took out the rough parts, to put it in the book" (6). In the traditional oral storytellers' versions, the "politically incorrect" aspects remain. Sobol writes that "within a traditional storytelling event, each person present would hear what they were willing or able to hear. If the children did not understand a certain reference, that was fine; there was plenty of action elsewhere to keep them busy" (9). As Sobol illustrates, the oral versions of the Jack Tales relied on action. The story happened; the events played out temporally. The storyteller acted out the tale from beginning to end; the story acted upon an audience assembled in a certain place at a certain time. Sobol explains that "far from obscuring the mythic themes of the tale, however, the obscenity and violence actually seemed, by intensified contrast, to heighten [the story's] power and mystery" (7). When the stories were set into print, they lost their temporal quality and became spatial in nature; any reader could skip backward or forward, be interrupted in mid-passage, and meditate upon certain words or phrases. What had been an interaction between a storyteller and an audience became instead a one-way message left by an author for any and all possible readers. The prudery (and marketing sense) of book publishers led the industry to take all readers into consideration—if one word or phrase is objectionable on a printed page, it will be present for all time. But the oral nature of the tales eliminates the existence of concrete evidence. The story only exists during the moment of telling and, therefore, has greater flexibility; it is an experience rather than a possession.

The longevity of "Jack and His Step-Dame" should not come as a surprise. It is a constructed narrative that has been interpreted and re-created as it passes through time. Like the other Jack Tales, it adapts over the centuries to fit the changing needs of the culture. When one version loses its cultural relevance—another is created to take its place. Each adaptation starts from the old story and encompasses the new conditions, but "Jack and His Step-Dame" still remains as the same basic story.

The most widely known Jack Tale is "Jack the Giant Killer," an international tale that has appeared in over thirty different countries. It is listed and numbered 328 in *The Types of the Folktale*,[3] an index begun by Antti Aarne and subsequently enlarged by Stith Thompson. The tale has been broken down into several subtypes. Aarne and Thompson describe them:

> I. expeditions to the Giant. (a) The hero sets out to steal from a giant in order to get revenge for former ill-treatment or (b) to help a friendly king, or (c) as a task suggested by jealous rivals, or (d) he ascends to the sky on a magic beanstalk and finds the giant's house. (119)

The motifs that Aarne and Thompson list demonstrate how Jack in his role as giant killer begins his quest. Further variations occur when "the giant killer" robs and then captures and/or kills the giant.

One of the prototypes for "Jack the Giant Killer" comes from the legend of King Arthur. Geoffrey of Monmouth's History of the Kings of Britain (1136) is the earliest surviving biography of the English king and describes how Arthur fights and kills a giant in a battle near Land's End. Six centuries later, Jack faces off against a giant at the same location. The opening of The History of Jack and the Giants begins "in the Reign of King Arthur, near the Land's End of England" (Opie and Opie, Classic Fairy Tales, 64). Textual "equivalence" does not always automatically confirm that there is a common narrative base in which both texts are grounded. In this case, however, certain elements are undoubtedly shared: indeed, both Arthur's name and the location of Land's End are highlighted in the first sentence. Noting the similarity, Lindahl asks if "the legendary British king [has] traded in his crown for a hoe and become a working class hero?" (xv).

Geoffrey of Monmouth's work is a mixture of factual information and fictional embellishments. The History of the Kings of Britain is not a chronicle of contemporary events, but a reconstruction of the past, using the scraps of evidence that were available. For example, Arthur's birth, which Merlin brings about by disguising Uther Pendragon as the husband of Igerna of Cornwall, is an echo of a similar tale in the romances about Alexander the Great. Arthur's "biography" seems to be made up of material borrowed from all kinds of sources. Geoffrey of Monmouth did not merely write a fictional history: he appropriated the necessary stories to produce a hero-king who was very much his readers' ideal.

Indeed, elements of the Arthurian legend date back further than the (speculative) date of Arthur's birth.[4]

Like many other types of oral narratives, aspects of Arthur's exploits may have been appropriated from a prior culture. For example, in The Encyclopedia of Arthurian Legends, Ronan Coghlan argues that the character of Arthur derives in part from the gods of Norse mythology. When the Anglo-Saxons invaded England, they brought with them their own oral traditions and mythological tales. Through the processes of intermarriage and assimilation, Coghlan believes the descendants of the Anglo-Saxons and the Britons may have adopted the stories and placed a British leader in the Norse gods' place (1-17). Similar types of appropriation can be ascribed to Jack as the culture's perception of an ideal hero is worked into his character by the tellers of his tales. Thus a hero of Arthur's stature—who is in fact a compilation of prior heroes—can become a working class hero named Jack.

A second prototype for "Jack the Giant Killer" also developed from Norse mythology. *The Prose Edda* (1220) of Snorri Sturluson details Thor's[5] journey to Utgard and his confrontation with the giant Skrymir, who is Utgard-Loki in disguise. In the legend, Utgard-Loki is suspicious of Thor. Before going to sleep, the giant makes a mound of earth to occupy his sleeping place. During the night Thor strikes the mound with his hammer, Mjollnir. Utgard-Loki complains that a leaf has fallen on his head. When Thor strikes again, Utgard-Loki believes an acorn has hit him. With Thor's final strike, the giant complains that a bird dropping has splashed across his face (Crossley-Holland 85-86).

A similar incident occurs in *The History of Jack and the Giants* (1711), which is one of the earliest surviving English versions of AT 328. When Jack rests for the night in the Giant's house, he takes the precaution of placing a thick billet in his bed while he hides in a dark corner of the room. The giant enters the room in the dead of night and strikes several heavy blows upon the bed:

> The next Morning Jack came to give him Thanks for his Lodging. Quoth the Giant, How have you rested? [D]id you not feel something in the Night?
>
> No, nothing, quoth Jack, but a Rat, which gave me three or four Slaps with her Tail. (Opie and Opie 69)

What the tales share is a common set of motifs denoting strength and cleverness; the two cultures seem to place high value on these traits. Both texts dwell on the physical attack and the deception that leads to escape. Yet the creation of each hero is culturally specific.

Thor and Jack represent "the giant killer" in their respective cultures. The stories present the heroes as psychologically complex, individualized figures who stand forth as the greatest, the strongest, or the smartest that the civilization has to offer. Yet the stories function on an allegorical level as well; the allegorical dimensions generalize the heroes' experience. One shifts continually between apprehending the character as an individual caught up in a particular situation and seeing within the situation a striking image which could apply to anyone within the culture.

The stories elaborate the cultural perspectives in great detail. For example, during the time when stories of Thor's exploits flourished, Germanic pre-Christian Europe was charged with strife. "A culture finds the [heroes] it needs," Crossley-Holland explains, "and the Norse world needed a [hero] to justify the violence that is one of its hallmarks" (xxv). Thor fit the culturally-defined image: he was huge, immensely strong, a bit slow on the uptake, easy to anger, fair, and dependable. He was the most beloved and respected of the gods that men invoked (Crossley-Holland xxvi).

Thor displays both the positive and the negative qualities of the culture from which he comes. His weakness (being slow on the uptake) is important largely because it hinders him. While tricked repeatedly by the giant, Thor is still not viewed as laughable. Crossley-Holland writes that "our sympathies remain with Thor because he is likeable, because he is being exploited, and because he represents the essential forces of law and order" (207). Thor's strength is the defining element of his character; it overshadows his negative attributes and helps him win the ultimate victory.

On the surface of the tales, both Thor and Jack follow the heroes' path established by AT 328: each man leaves his civilized home for a strange and magical wilderness where he encounters a series of trials, some of which he fails; eventually he returns, somewhat matured, to his home. But this is where the similarities between the two characters end. Although he is labeled "the giant killer," Jack has more in common with Utgard-Loki than he does with Thor.

For example, while Thor initiates the attack on the giant and depends upon his strength to resolve the situation, Jack is the recipient of the attack by the giant and uses his wits to prevail against a physically stronger opponent. This shift in the narrative implies a shift in the values of society. Thor is strong, but he is not bright—Utgard-Loki tricks him several times. On the other hand, since Jack is physically weak compared to the giant, he cannot afford to be attacked—one wrong move and he will forfeit his life. He uses an intellectual approach to trick the giant. In the culture that created Jack, cleverness is of more value than strength. Ordinary people who could not hope to become as strong as a giant (lacking the proper genetic code) could see themselves learning enough to trick their opponent.

Prior to the publication of *The History of Jack and the Giants*, stories about giants were part of the English popular culture. In *The Classic Fairy Tales*, Opie and Opie admit that there was a wide distribution of tales concerning the bamboozling of giants and other fearful creatures (59). Along with the *History of the Kings of Britain* and Sir Thomas Malory's *Le Morte D'Arthur* (1485), *The Complaynt of Scotland* (1549) discusses the problems with giants who threaten mankind.

In the sixteenth and seventeenth centuries in England, references to "Jack the Giant Killer" began appearing in prose and drama. A variation of the rhyme that is typically associated with the giant—"Fi, fie, fo, fum,/I smell the blood of an Englishman"—first appears in Thomas Nashe's *Have With You Saffron-Walden* (1596). In 1605, the same rhyme, with slightly different wording, is found at the end of Act Three, Scene Four, of Shakespeare's *The Tragedy of King Lear*. It is true that the character of Jack is never mentioned as the giant's foe in these two works; however, Nashe, at least, utilizes "Jack" as the main character in an earlier work, *The Unfortunate Traveler: or, The Life of Jack Wilton* (1594). Jack Wilton bears a striking resemblance to the "trickster Jack" of certain Jack Tales. In particular, Jack Wilton's exploits with the cider merchant echo the same sort of playful and good-natured trickery that occurs in "Jack and the Heifer Hide."

Lindahl believes that Jack "had become the John Doe of English oral tradition" by the eighteenth century (xvi). For example, the name of Jack appears sixteen times in *The Oxford Dictionary of Nursery Rhymes* while most other male names appear only five times.[6] These rhymes were one of the most popular forms of oral entertainments and first appeared in broad distribution at the same time the chapbooks featuring Jack's exploits began mass publication. In fact, Jack was a favored name for characters in all types of literature (Lindahl xvi).

"Jack's popularity grew throughout Britain," Lindahl continues, "at the same time Britain was colonizing the world"(xvi). Beyond England's borders the British influence on oral narratives often appeared in the form of Jack Tales. In Scotland he appears as "Jock," and in Ireland he is known as "Jake." He is referred to by both "Jack" and "John" in the early African American folktales.

By the early nineteenth century, the focus of AT 328 had shifted from portraying Jack as a giant killer to offering him to the public as a great adventurer who had dared to climb the beanstalk, enter unfamiliar territory, and find unbelievable riches. (The fact that there was a giant at the top of the beanstalk seemed to be understood.) The title Jack and the Beanstalk began to appear more frequently in publications: *The History of Jack and the Bean Stalk* (1820), published by Francis Orr and Sons, was closely followed by *Jack and the Bean-Stalk: A New Version* (1848), from Wm. J. Reynolds and Co., *The Wonderful Tale of Jack and the Bean Stalk* (1860), from E.C. Bennett, and subsequent editions of *Jack and the Beanstalk* by R. Andre (1888), E. Nesbit (1908), and Captain Edric Vredenberg (1919).

Along with the shift in title came a shift in the character and motivation of Jack as he set about his task of giant-killing. Earlier versions of Jack the Giant Killer had Jack begin his quest on a directive from the King:

> [Jack] humbly requested the King his master, to fit him forth with a horse and money to travel in search of strange and new adventures: For, saith he, there are many Giants yet living in the remote parts of this kingdom, and the dominion of Wales; to the unspeakable damage of your majesty's liege subjects; wherefore...I doubt not but in a short time to cut them off root and

branch, and so rid the realm of these cruel Giants. (Opie and Opie, Classic Fairy Tales 72)

In the earlier versions, Jack had a legitimate excuse to attack the giant; his sovereign assigned him to rid the kingdom of beings who were causing "unspeakable damage" to the king's liege subjects. Jack's motives for the quest centered around duty and honor—not on the profit he could glean from the giant's holdings.

The element of the noble quest slowly disappeared from the adaptations of AT 328. By 1943, when Chase published his version of "Jack and the Bean Tree," Jack undertakes the journey to the giant's land because he is bored with his home life and he kills the giant to retrieve a greater amount of plunder. To conceal the fact of outright theft, Chase has Jack explain that "the bean tree was his'n and that ever'thing on it belonged to him" (36).

There is no textual evidence to suggest that the giant in the story deserves this treatment. Unlike the giant in the "Giant-Killer" versions, he has not destroyed any towns, pillaged any farmsteads, or eaten any villagers. The acceptance of a (relatively) blameless being in the role of a maligned creature reflects a shift in cultural perceptions; the giant's crime, Yolen suggests in *Touch Magic*, is the unforgivable—he owns a large property and expensive items while remaining undeniably a giant (106).

In Chase's tale, Jack's behavior toward the giant reveals that the giant is viewed as a cultural outsider. Jack steals the giant's possessions, lies to the giant's wife, and murders the giant without a single qualm. Yolen explains:

> The audience is lulled into accepting such bad behavior because—we are told—the one upon whom such depravities are visited is only [a giant]. And [giants], after all, do not deserve our pity. (106)

Chase portrays the giant as the ultimate outsider. In the context of the story, it is not only morally right to steal his property and then to kill him, but, as Yolen reveals, it is virtually incumbent upon Jack to do so (106). His actions are entirely heroic within the scope of the tale.

"The Giant-Killer" tends to alter subtly according to the culture in which he is operating and mirrors the concerns of the day. "The stories and characters take on a protective coloration from the surrounding culture," Sobol remarks in "The Jack Tales: Coming From Afar," which "is at the heart of the cycle's enduring power" (15). By the time Chase presented his version of AT 328, the narrative had gradually moved away from the accepted English theme of duty to king and country and, instead, had focused on the material possessions to be gleaned from an adventure. Chase makes the persuasive argument that the "Appalachian Jack" is an uniquely American hero: "our Appalachian giant-killer has acquired the easy-going, unpretentious rural American manners that make him so different from his English cousin, the cocksure, dashing young hero of the 'fairytale'"(ix). The cultural climate had changed once again, and Jack adapted to become an Appalachian/American hero.

Jack has stubbornly retained his place at the forefront of the oral traditions of the west. Over the centuries the parameters of the Jack Tales have been redrawn, Jack's dilemmas have been reshaped, and his character has changed—but he has endured each reincarnation with something of the original stories intact. Jack has an adaptability that is undeniable—and his status as the symbol for the common man stems directly from this adaptability. Jack takes on those traits which are most admired; his intellectual and moral preoccupations reflect those of the culture at large; and he dramatizes a society's reality in an imaginative way.

The history of the Jack Tales is the story of their refashioning. Storytellers take from their predecessors the aspects of the tale they can best use for themselves, adapting their narratives for different times and cultures. The Jack Tales offer various possibilities to different cultures. Indeed, the Jack Tales can be understood only when their placement in a culture is understood. Critics almost have to function like anthropologists by studying the sources, examining surviving evidence, and interpolating the cultural and social history out of which the tales are produced.

Even though Chase had tried to distance the Appalachian Jack Tales from their European predecessors, it is important to note that the two traditions remain connected. The Appalachian storytellers employ, more or less extensively, the materials, ideas, and form of the earlier successful texts. In many of the stories, the narrative units (characters, events, motivations, consequences, context, imagery, and so forth) remain similar to the European versions. Yet there is no question that the Appalachian tellers have successfully created their own adaptations of the Jack Tales. The adaptations reflect the aesthetic system of their particular era and that era's cultural needs and pressures.

In the end it is Jack's enduring presence and tenacious survival that must be admired. Most Indo-European languages and cultures can boast their own addition to the vast collection of The Jack Tales. The different cultural adaptations reinforce the generality of the Jack Tales, their potential for wide and varied appeal; in short, their existence as a continuing form or archetype. Jack's nature is inclusive and universal; wherever there is a fictional giant to slay, he steps into the breech.

2

The Storyteller From Beech Mountain: Ray Hicks And Traditional Appalachian Jack Tales

"The storyteller is the figure in which the righteous man encounters himself."

—Walter Benjamin

When Richard Chase traveled through the Appalachian Mountains and became the first to collect Jack Tales, Ray Hicks was still a child. Because Hicks had no recourse to written versions of the tales, he belongs to the last generation of Appalachian storytellers remaining truly oral. He did not learn of the Jack Tales from books, but primarily from his grandparents, Benjamin and Julie Hicks. As Robert Isbell relates in *The Last Chivaree*, a biography of the Hicks family of Beech Mountain, Hicks (even before he was of an age to attend school) would walk the half mile to his grandparents' farm and help them with the daily chores of chopping kindling, shelling beans, fetching water, and sweeping the yard. The reward for his labors would be the stories and ballads of ages past (39). In an interview with Barbara McDermitt, Hicks says of his grandparents:

> See, I'd sit down with em and let em tell the tale. An[d] say, "tell that again, I'd like to learn how to tell hit." Then I'd ask em a question what hit meant. And that was the reason hit got on up. (4)

After a short period of time Hicks joined his grandparents in performance and told his own stories. As Isbell relates, before his formal education began, Hicks could narrate long, complex tales (39). "I've been telling these stories," Hicks explains, "since my Grandpa Benjamin passed them on to me when I was a little boy shelling thrash beans on his porch" (Isbell 32).

Under these circumstances Hicks began his life-long fascination with storytelling and the Jack Tales. He became more intimately involved with "Jack" than a person who merely read about the adventures in a book would have. "For me its inherited, I think," Hicks claims, "inherited in the people" (McDermitt 4). The voices and accumulated wisdom of his grandparents are intertwined with the oral narratives—as are the voices of the Hicks ancestors stretching out through the generations—and echo in Ray Hicks's renditions of the tales.

Being involved in the tradition of oral storytelling has not only shaped Hicks's life, but has allowed him to have an impact upon his native region. In this chapter I will undertake my own analysis of the storytelling methods of Ray Hicks and explore his special influence on the Jack Tales.

JACK REPRESENTS A COMMUNITY

Since his birth in 1922, Hicks has spent almost his entire life in the two-story frame farmhouse built by his father, Nathan Hicks, in 1914. The house, with a rusty tin roof and walls painted only with the patina of time, is currently the oldest dwelling on Beech Mountain. A large porch wraps around the outside and it hosts benches, chairs, and a stack of firewood. Inside there are few modern conveniences; Hicks' wife, Rosa, cooks on the wood burning stove that also provides heat for the home. Long wooden planks worn smooth through years of scuffing cover the floors and hand-made furniture fills the rooms. Echoes of his home fill the tales that he tells.

Like the house, the immediate environs of Beech Mountain have not changed much since Hicks was a child. The house remains isolated—the nearest neighbor lives a half mile away through the forest and fields. Modern entertainments, like television and movie theaters, are recent innovations to the area. On Beech Mountain, storytelling, singing, and music played on homemade instruments are still the preferred activities. In an interview with Jimmy Neil Smith, Hicks explains:

> When I was a-growing up, that's all the entertainment we'd have, a tellin' stories. When us youngins would git together and git a little rough, somebody would start one of them [Jack] tales. One would take a part, and all of us kids would quiet down and you could hear a pin drop. (4)

The stories may have originally been told to entertain the children, but they also served as a way to bond family members together and create an underlying dimension of community. The Jack Tales were something of their own—something that belonged strictly to the people of Beech Mountain and reflected their interests and their lives.

The tales promoted a type of ethnocentricism that is not unusual for an orally-based community. In *Orality and Literacy*, Walter Ong suggests that the orally-based transmission of knowledge contributes to a type of isolationist behavior within a community. Unlike written literature, oral art forms do not allow the storage of knowledge as an entity separate from the larger community (42). "Oral cultures," Ong believes, "must conceptualize and verbalize all their knowledge with more or less close reference to the human life-world" (42). Oral knowledge exists without annals, lists, or databases; the knowledge derives from the mental ecology of the community (41-42).

For example, the Jack Tales from Beech Mountain exist in an isolated sphere—essentially in the mountains of North Carolina—and contain little reference to the geography or customs of other areas. Jack may travel a good deal in his stories, but he rarely reaches a place in which the landscape differs from the narrator's home. Jack may even visit a place as mythical as a king's castle, only to find that the "castle" is actually a well-kept frame farmhouse with a front porch.[7] Even when keeping the traditional elements in the tales, storytellers on Beech Mountain adapt the elements to mirror their own experiences.

This prioritizing of knowledge leads to a certain type of discourse—a traditional and a conservative one that demands continuity. The discourse encompasses what is concrete and familiar within a community and does not often reach far beyond its prescribed boundaries. Ong believes that this limitation leads to a formalization of the "story" concepts used to pass on the accumulated knowledge of such a society, and that this knowledge is acquired through participation and repetition (41-57). For this reason, the story not only is interiorized by the participants but the boundaries of communal knowledge are reinforced.

In his adaptations of the Jack Tales, Hicks includes not only the community-sanctioned versions of the kings and their castles, he also maintains the rhetoric used by his grandparents and great-grandparents. Long after certain words and phrases have disappeared from the general vocabulary of the mountains, Hicks uses them in his tales to set the proper image for his listeners. For example, he utilizes "bairn" for "born," "steer" for "oxen," and "legal" for "money." As Isbell illustrates, Hicks's manner of speaking has retained the vivid expressions used in the days of his great-grandparents and can be traced back to the first settlers to arrive from England in the sixteenth century (6). In *The Storytellers' Journey*, Kathryn Windham comments that "you have to get into Ray's rhythms and speech patterns before you really understand what he is saying" (Sobol 134). Many believe that Hicks, as one of the last storytellers to learn the Jack Tales in a purely oral setting, is the last mountain man to speak an evolved form of Elizabethan English (Isbell 36).

As Ong explains, the language used by oral artists does not necessarily mirror the general language of the area in which they live. Words and expressions are passed down through the generations and have specific connotations within the realm of storytelling (23). In *The Singer of Tales*, Albert B. Lord illustrates that words and phrases that remain in the narratives long after having passed out of the general language reflect the linguistic, social, and political history of the area (49). Specific words and phrases help both to remind listeners of their cultural past and to appeal to their social conditioning—their traditions, their customs, and their common heritage.

In addition to their entertainment value and their function in structuring a tight social bond, these stories, through creation and repetition, represent an outlet for the accumulated knowledge and wisdom of a society. Always, those who remember the history and traditions of the community receive great veneration. Ong explains that, in an orally-based community, "knowledge is hard to come by and precious, and society regards highly those wise old men and women who specialized in conserving it, who know and can tell the stories of the days of old" (41). In some instances, their transmission of this knowledge can mean the difference between life and death.

Hicks believes that "I wouldn't have been livin, probably, if I'd not been Jack's friend" (McDermitt 9). The information contained in the tales provided him with the necessary tools of survival. For instance, one day during his tenth year, Hicks was caught out in the open by a blizzard. The snow and wind were so fierce that he could not catch his breath, but he remembered some of the Jack Tales his grandfather had told and put the information to practical use:

> My clothes was no good and the wind would blow through them and just take my breath. I'd just dive my head in a snow drift till I could breathe. Just like Grandpa Benjamin told me. After ducking down to catch my breath I'd come back up, and the wind would cut through me again. Gah, the wind in this country's sharp and blowing. (Isbell 73-74)

Hicks was in real danger of freezing to death on the mountain, but the knowledge contained in the Jack Tales helped him to survive.

20   Ray Hicks and the Jack Tales

In creating his story adaptations, Hicks attempts to interweave truths and myths passed down through the generations. Tales may begin in the mundane world of Beech Mountain, focusing on the trials and tribulations of hunger and despair that come from living in such an economically blighted rural community, but they may end in feasts and triumphs of mythic proportions.

Hicks's stories mirror both the stressful conditions of life and the inspirational dreams of the citizens in his home area. For instance, Hicks's adaptation of "The Heifer Hide" (transcribed by W.F.H. Nicolaisen in "The Teller and the Tale: Storytelling on Beech Mountain") suggests the isolation of farm life and the temptations that occur there. In Hicks's tale, Jack begins his life in abject poverty and he must set out on the road to seek his fortune or risk starving to death. When night falls and Jack requires lodgings, a farmer's wife grudgingly admits him into her home. She provides scant food for the traveler and quickly ushers him upstairs to sleep. Because of his undiminished hunger, Jack cannot rest comfortably. Finding a rat hole in the floor to spy on the farmer's wife, he watches as she prepares for an illicit male caller (Nicolaisen 137). Hicks recounts:

> [Jack] 'gin to hunt over in there a found a rat hole.
> And when he looked down there through it, one eye wanderin', directly he looked in there, and there was the eating table—old time eating table.
> And imagine, down there was a man with a big suit o' clothes on and a black high topped hat—ten-gallon hat—and was a suitable lookin' man, young ma—middle-aged man.
> And he says, "Man, I'm gonna watch."
> And he kept watchin', And directly they took hands, went and danced around the table.
> She went to the cupboard and got out hog meat and beef and chicken meat. Eat some of that.
> Then him and her took hands and danced around the table agin.
> She went and got old timey fruitcake and pumpkin pie, Then eat some of it, and took hands and danced around the table.
> And she went to the cupboard and brought out pure corn whiskey and wine—it was aged: it had turned brown.
> And one glass was all you'd a needed to make you kick a, runnin'—of that wine, one drinkin' glass full.
> And so, he said, when they drunk, got whiskey and wine, they took hands and, said, boys they did dance a buck dance around that table. (Nicolaisen 137-138)

The ethnocentricism of the area extends even to Hicks's imaginary feast. As Isbell explains, Hicks would rarely eat in a restaurant, and when he did, he found the food lacking in taste and quality (31). The food is presented for the narrator's pleasure and lists nothing out of the ordinary for Beech Mountain cooking. Mentioning hog meat, beef, chicken, old timey fruitcake, pumpkin pie, whiskey, and wine, Hicks creates a veritable culinary feast in his tale (one that most listeners realize Jack will somehow consume before the tale's end). While evoking a meal that makes Jack's mouth water, Hicks's description of the "old timey" and home-cooked food has a similar effect upon his listeners.

The passage also centers upon the common fears of Hicks's boyhood community—the temptation of adultery and the destruction of the family bond. After each course is consumed, Hicks provides a repetition so obvious that it immediately catches the listener's attention. In each instance the couple takes hands and dances around the table. The repetition suggests that the world of the tale is too patterned to be realistic. Hicks comments that the stories "ain't really to believe because a lot in them ain't true; but when you're listening, you got to believe" (Isbell 32-33). The story is not true; it never actually happened. In effect, Hicks is challenging his audience through the use of the repetitive phrases to focus clearly on the actions being performed and to highlight their underlying meaning.

During the early and mid-twentieth century, people living on Beech Mountain were mainly subsistence farmers. They grew potatoes, corn, and cabbage and had few luxuries. As Isbell relates, the farmers had no "cash crops." If a man needed to earn money, he would have to hire himself out as a laborer; that meant traveling to the site of the job and perhaps remaining away from home for weeks at a time (67-68). Such separation could place a strain upon marriages and families.

During this time it was also not unusual for traveling preachers to visit the farmsteads. "You see," Hicks recalls, preachers "moved from one meetinghouse to another. Most of them didn't light in one place like us; they'd ride horses or mules from way off" (Isbell 40). In "The Heifer Hide," the absence of a husband and the visit of a "well-dressed man" (a description traditionally employed of a preacher) to a farm reflects the concerns of the community in regards to adultery.

Hicks does not use a word-for-word repetition, but the phrase "took hands and danced" is essentially the same. The two people join together and dance around a table covered with food that the wife has hidden from her husband. The phrase "took hands and danced" is an allusion to sexual behavior—a device often employed by storytellers when confronted with crowds consisting of mixed genders and ages. In this instance, however, the image created by Hicks emphasizes the wife's betrayal of her family. Not only does she give herself to the preacher, she also gives away food intended for the family.

22   Ray Hicks and the Jack Tales

The selfishness of the farmer's wife also mirrors certain family practices Hicks encountered as a child. As Isbell explains, when the Hicks family had visitors and there was too little food to go around, the children often had to go without a meal. As a youngster, Hicks believed this to be unjust (45). "How come," Hicks had asked his sister, "every time people come, Mama uses the wood I chopped to cook the vittles, but you and me and the [other children] don't get to eat?" (Isbell 45). This belief is reinforced later in the tale when the husband challenges the wife and she claims that she is saving the food for her family. In fact, when the husband tries to take anything, she calls up a litany of grandfathers, half-sisters, and first cousins to defend her position (Nicolaisen 141). In Hicks's view this is false justification. Families should come first, but the wife's so-called family exists only to provide an excuse for her hording.

In order to assist the audience in locating the truth behind the surface of the story, Hicks provides the repetitions necessary to establish a humorous situation. The first repetition of the phrase "took hands and danced" creates a somewhat exaggerated notion of the couple's sexual appetite (seemingly matched by their appetite for food) and leads the audience to a moment of humor. By the third repetition, Hicks has made it quite evident that the primary focus of the farmer's wife and the preacher is their insatiable desires for food and sex. In case any doubt remains, Hicks provides a final repetition and includes another reference to sexuality—the buck dance.[8]

The repetitions prepare the listeners for the humorous situation that develops in the tale—the wife's desperation to hide her adultery and to save her lover—and provide a safe enough distance to allow the comical elements to shine through. The repetitions also serve to highlight both the wife's treachery toward her husband—and toward family life in general—and her lack of hospitality; this behavior lends a moral justification to Jack for tricking the wife into providing him an excellent meal.

The trickster is an important aspect of the Appalachian Jack Tales. In trickster folklore a poor and supposedly powerless individual plays tricks or pranks on the rich and seemingly powerful people within a society. With his rebellious nature and his tendency to bend social mores to his own advantage, the trickster seems to lead an enviable life. Richard Endoes and Alfonas Ortez, in *American Indian Myths and Legends*, argue that the North American trickster "not only represents some primordial creativity from our earlier days, but he…[also] represents the potency of…freedom—a nothingness that makes something of itself" (335). The trickster character will survive any situation, but he may need to use his wits in order to "create" an opportunity to acquire what he needs.

During the early part of the twentieth century, some inhabitants of Beech Mountain objected to "trickster Jack" stories. Hicks reveals that some members of the community had believed that the tales "oughtn't to be allowed [because Jack] he done them things, cheating people…they feared the children would learn to cheat and outsmart people" (McDermitt 6). Hicks has always refuted statements that describe Jack's tricks in a negative way. He comments:

> I think Jack was a whole lot like that, in some of the tales. Now you see they all tell it different. In the sense it was goin in. Was do good for evil and not turn railin fer railin. An Jack I think like I said, he was the kind of a man if ye hit him on one cheek, he'd just turn the othern, and say, hit it. And then he'd just charge around there, an then outsmart em, and git it back! Is the way I think Jack was now. Outsmarted em. (McDermitt 6)

Hicks's Jack Tales center on a trickster who is not necessarily a cheater, but rather a clever character who outsmarts the people who try to harm him or his friends.

Two types of trickster characters predominate in Hicks's narratives. The first type Hicks describes as a "Jesse James" type who robs from the rich to give to the poor (McDermitt 8). Hicks's description also brings to mind images of Robin Hood. In the narratives, Jack's character is comparable to the legendary tricksters who defend the weak and stand up for what is right and noble. Hicks's second type of trickster character is more morally ambiguous than that of the "defender." This is the "Jack" who is concerned with survival at any cost and will do anything—including killing giants or robbing thieves—to prolong his own life.

At first the characters may not appear to be "heroic" in the traditional sense, yet Hicks's tricksters follow Vladimir Propp's definition of heroes from *Morphology of the Folktale*. Propp suggests that there are two types of heroes: "seeker" heroes who alleviate the suffering or misfortunes of others and "victim" heroes who suffer directly from the actions of the villains (36-38).

The "heroes" are the building blocks out of which the Jack Tales are constructed. Hicks defines the trickster in terms of his polar opposite. In the *Course in General Linguistics*, Ferdinand de Saussure posits the idea that there is a structure, a set of relationships in the narrative, that gives it meaning (117). The basic polarity involves the relationship between the trickster and the villain and provides much of the "heroic" content to Jack's character. The action of the trickster can actually be interpreted in terms of the counter-actions by the opposing character. The trickster is everything that the villain is not: their actions both have meaning because of the opposition.

24   Ray Hicks and the Jack Tales

Hicks's tale "Unlucky Jack and Lucky Jack" (transcribed by McDermitt) is an example of Propp's "seeker" hero. The story provides an example of the beneficial behavior of the trickster to the weaker members of the community. The narrative begins with a farmer hiring Unlucky Jack and forcing him to work without food or pay. Unlucky Jack also has to agree to submit to a lashing if he ever becomes angry. Because he signs a contract he does not understand, Unlucky Jack ends up working until he almost drops from starvation; when he grows angry at the ill-treatment, the farmer lacerates Unlucky Jack's back. Now the trickster, Lucky Jack, enters the tale and finds his friend bleeding to death on the road. Lucky Jack carries Unlucky Jack to the doctor and saves his life (McDermitt 19-20).

At this point in the narrative, Hicks insists that Lucky Jack's good nature shines through. "Jack [is] an upright man," he explains, but also cautions that "in other ways he [is] pretty rough…There are lots of people like that. Would do you bad in ways. When it comes that you [are] helpless, they'd help ye quicker than one of the others" (McDermitt 7).

After tending to his friend, Lucky Jack applies for employment at the same farm. His first assignment is to tend the sheep; to keep himself fed, Lucky Jack kills one animal each day. Yet the farmer refuses to become angry and merely re-assigns Lucky Jack to plowing. The boy makes a mess of the fields and trades one of the draft horses for a donkey that he later "accidentally" kills. The farmer still refuses to admit that he is angry and assigns Lucky Jack to pick apples (McDermitt 20-21).

Instead of climbing the ladder to harvest the apples, Lucky Jack starts cutting down the trees. The farmer observes this and decides to demonstrate the proper way to pick apples. After he climbs into the tree, Lucky Jack removes the ladder and refuses to replace it until the farmer provides a meal. The farmer agrees and yells to his wife to feed Lucky Jack, but the trickster makes her believe that she has to kiss him. When the farmer realizes this, he becomes angry and attacks Lucky Jack, but the trickster is too wily and manages to lacerate his enemy's back (McDermitt 21-22).

The trickster's heroic qualities are revealed through his actions as he becomes the polar opposite of the farmer. "Back in the old days in the mountains," Hicks reports, "people were taught more of the Old Testament law than they are now. People was teached an eye fer an eye and a tooth fer a tooth, an so that made Jack raised up like that" (McDermitt 7-8). The trickster demonstrates a defense against the machinations of strangers. Lucky Jack plays "Jesse James" in the story and extracts from the villainous farmer the "eye for an eye" on Unlucky Jack's behalf.

Hicks's rendition of "Unlucky Jack and Lucky Jack" is, among other things, a record of the Beech Mountain community seeking ways to adjust itself to the terrible economic blight that had invaded the area. The members of the community found themselves living in a world whose financial demands they were wholly unprepared to meet. As Isbell explains, when the Great Depression hit the United States, it caused great difficulty for the farmers of Beech Mountain, but the reasons behind this misfortune might well have remained a mystery. The market for the natural resources of the area was controlled by industrialists and financiers outside of the community and, although the farmers toiled hard, they were ill-rewarded for their efforts (58).

This was a crucial moment in the history of the region. The men of Beech Mountain were very much aware that they needed legal currency in order to survive, and one of their only outlets for employment was signing contracts to hire on as laborers outside of the community. All those suffering from a lack of funds shared a common demoralization, but it was perhaps worse among the farmers who were deprived of the small but important sense of self-sufficiency that they had previously enjoyed.

The fear of thievery loomed large. Many of the men could not read very well and would have trouble defending their rights against a contract they could not understand. It is true that a consciousness of improvement through formal learning had swept the area, but the modest advances in education had not affected the current generation of farmers. Indeed, as he explains to Smith, Hicks did not attend school past the seventh grade and passed simply because he had been helpful to the teacher by keeping the stove working during the winter (7).

The need to find employment and to enter into contractual obligations without being able to understand exactly what they were signing bred a sense of helplessness among the men of Beech Mountain that is reflected in "Unlucky Jack and Lucky Jack." And, perhaps worst of all, the men had to seek this work from strangers who were indifferent to the fate of the Beech Mountain families. It is no accident that the "farmer" in Hicks's narrative is never formally named—he is representative of the nameless outside forces that have gained economic control over the home community. It is also no accident that the stories are not affiliated with any movement to bring public opinion to bear on the government or other centers of power. The Appalachian tales are firmly fixed in their social orientation; it is the inhabitants and their ways of life that form the principle concern. They are the people for whom the oral stories are composed and whose interests and tastes determine their tone and content. Thus a man who needs to hire out as a laborer and who hears the stories cannot avoid hearing his own personal situation in the narrative and may find alternatives to his own problems.

In Appalachia, the Jack Tales have always subjected contemporary problems to a continuous process of analysis and criticism. Perhaps this is one reason why the stories have had such an effect—reaching far beyond mere entertainment. As Hicks comments, "it takes Jack to live" (McDermitt 9).

THE STORYTELLER BECOMES HIS CHARACTER

The second type of trickster character in the Jack Tales seems to rise out of the ever-present poverty of the mountains and the continuous struggle of its inhabitants to stay alive. Hicks's own personal experience is also included in the tales. "What we had at home was good," Hicks explains to Isbell, "but there was never enough [food]" (45). Much of Hicks's childhood was spent in search of edible things in order to avoid starvation. Although a lot of people could have helped Hicks alleviate his hunger and might have assisted him through this rough time, he was ignored. "It was tough," he shares. "You had to do things to live that your heart's desire or your conscience didn't want to do because…food was so light" (McDermitt 8).

When Hicks was twelve years old, he found a large pile of rutabagas next to a corn field. Having had nothing to eat for the last two days, he took one. The farmer caught him and forbid him from ever passing by his farm again (Isbell 66). Hicks recounts:

> Wouldn't hurt em at all. They wouldn't let me tech it. Well, that's where Jack comes in. A lot of times you have to go get it, slip and get it, if you [are to] live. Hit [the Bible] says, ask first fer everything ye git, but I'll tell anybody one thing if you have to ask fer everything ye git ye'll live hard cause there ain't enough of em to let ye have hit. They won't see it right. (McDermitt 8)

In Hicks's view, the farmer could have spared one rutabaga to feed a starving child because death stalked closer to the boy than to the man. The farmer, however, did not view the situation in this fashion, so this is "where Jack comes in."

Hicks's version of "The Doctor's Daughter" or "Jack and the Robbers" (transcribed by McDermitt), illustrates Propp's "victim" hero. The tale rises out of Hicks's own desperate poverty as a child and the lack of charity among certain members of the community. While the trickster and his parents share-crop on the doctor's farm, Jack falls in love with the doctor's daughter. The doctor requires any prospective bridegrooms to be in possession of a thousand guineas before he will allow his daughter to be courted. In response to this, Jack decides to leave home and seek his fortune and, after many days of travel is so weak and hungry that he takes shelter in the house of some robbers. They find him and threaten to shoot him unless he steals three steers from a local farmer. Jack acquires the cattle through a series of tricks and the robbers are so pleased with him that they give him the thousand guineas so he can marry the doctor's girl (9-13).

Hicks believes that Jack is justified in his actions:

> Now robbin, that ain't God's law to rob somebody out of their work...Well now Jack, what I was-a-meaning, he didn't go and bare face rob nobody, ye see. He talked them out of it. That's what I'm getting to. Jack didn't go in an pull a gun on em an say give me that. Like the robbers told him, he had to steal the steer to save his life or the robbers would kill him. The three farmer's steers. Jack wasn't a man like the robbers was, holding a gun...Jack just took it by talkin hit out of em. He wouldn't hurt nobody. He ain't wanted to steal the steers. He just got caught in it. Course that farmer needed his oxen paid bad, him and his wife and children. Probably had several children. And they needed it bad. Well Jack needed it too. Worse than he [the farmer] did because he was going to get killed. (8)

"The Doctor's Daughter" or "Jack and the Robbers" mirrors Hicks predicament with the theft of the rutabaga. As with Jack and the three steers, he needed the rutabaga more than the farmer. The basic polarity involves the relationship between the trickster and stingy farmer. In both cases, justification lies with the person closer to death.

Yet even the trickster character will accept death if he believes his actions will help the members of his community. In "Whickety-Whack, Into My Sack" (a story that provides a mixture of the two trickster characters), Jack is a soldier who left the army after thirty years of service. He meets a beggar on the road and offers to divide his food—two loaves of bread—with the man. Farther on down the road he meets a second beggar and divides his food a second time, planning on giving the second man only half a loaf of bread. Jack feels bad about this transaction—reasoning that since he gave the first beggar a full loaf, the second beggar must be entitled to the same amount—so he gives the whole loaf to the second man. Because of his honesty, the beggar presents Jack with a magical sack that will hold anything and a magical glass that allows a person to see death (Hicks 10).

28   Ray Hicks and the Jack Tales

After a few adventures, Jack finds a man who owns a haunted farm. The farmer is willing to give the house and some of the land to any person who can remove the evil spirits. Jack volunteers and uses the sack to capture the six devils who have invaded the farm. Because he is threatened with death at their hands, Jack has justification for following the actions of the second type of trickster character and capturing and killing the devils (Hicks 11-12).

After he establishes himself on the farm, Jack hears that the king's daughter is deathly ill. The trickster sits at her bedside and watches his glass until he sees death approaching, then catches the specter in his sack. The king offers to pay Jack, but he will not accept any money (12-13). "I didn't come for wealth. I come to save your daughter," Jack insists, revealing that his motives are those of the first type of trickster character (13). Here, there is no selfishness in his deeds. Hicks comments that when a person is in life-threatening danger, Jack will help without the incentive of a reward (McDermitt 7).

But later in the tale we find that Jack's trick has other consequences. Indeed, the death of the trickster occurs because the community needs his help in another way. Hicks narrates:

> [Jack] saw it was an old woman who'd just went to bones and hide. Her bones was a-creakin' as she walked, and her nose was a-bumpin' her knees. Jack says, "Howdy do, ma'am." "Howdy do," she says. "Law me, I can't git around no more. I'm so poor. I've just went to bones and hide. It seems like I've been a-livin' a million years. And I can't die. I've heerd that some rascal has Death tied up in a sack, and we can't die." (13)

After tying death up in the sack, Jack had a long and prosperous life. Now, it seemed, his trick had backfired and caused more harm than good in the community. Although he realizes that it means his own death, the trickster decides to open the sack. Hicks recounts that "they said when Jack opened it, he was the first one that fell dead. And that was the end of Jack in that tale" (13). In some instances, it seems that the good of the community outweighs the life of one individual, even if that individual is the trickster.

Hicks had a hard, grim childhood whose primary purpose, year after year, was to extract the bare essentials of diet and clothing from field and pasture. When he narrates a Jack Tale, he realizes that its value extends past the imaginative plot into an influence of community thought and action. On a certain level the stories make sense only as part of the linguistic and social code of a particular time and place. "I guess that's why I was put here," Hicks explains, "to tell the stories, to let people know how they can live...if it ever comes to that again" (Isbell 164).

Hicks's purpose in telling the tales follows a basic rule—he wants to help others in his community understand both past hardships and triumphs in order to promote their own survival. His work is meant to be didactic; the necessary skills of survival are embodied in the characters and plots. The experience of listening to the tales causes the audience members not only to learn about Jack's "tricks," but to be able to emulate them. The characters form mirrors in which the listeners may fashion themselves. At the same time, the characters have faults and make mistakes that the listeners need to understand and judge—a sympathetic experience that is practice for living.

Like many of his stories, Hicks's version of "Jack and the Northwest Wind" is semi-autobiographical. In an interview with Isbell, he admits that his life is part of the story; it includes "things I've done and seen…like when Jack and his mother were seeing it hard" (30). Events in the story mirror Hicks's experience as a child:

> Now, Jack and his Mama was together in the old log cabin. The cabin he was raised in. But his brothers was married off and gone. His father was deceased…left him and the mama with just an old poleaxe. With that axe he tried to cut wood for the mudrock fireplace. (Isbell 80-81)

As a child, Hicks was the primary caregiver for his ailing mother, who was never in good health and had to stay in bed most of the time. His father, Nathan, having all but abandoned the family, left the others to live well below the poverty line. "He'd give up," Hicks explains. "He got broke up in his nerves" (Isbell 74). At ten years of age, Hick became almost solely responsible for the welfare of his mother and younger siblings; and, because he was an intricate part of the family's survival, he could only attend school intermittently (Isbell 77). Like Jack, Hicks faced the responsibility of providing food, clothing, shelter, and heat for the family.

One winter day Hicks could not return home from school because a blizzard struck the region. The following day, he finally reached his home and found total desolation; Nathan Hicks had left and the family had no food or firewood. Hicks's mother and younger siblings were huddled in the bitterly cold house under their blankets (Isbell 74). In "Jack and the Northwest Wind," Hicks relates:

> The wind, where they stayed at, that Northwest wind…yah, hit would come through the house…like I've had it here…just burn the house…and Jack said,

"Me'n my mom ain't got nothing to eat much—no vittles, and we's about to starve, and hit so cold." (Isbell 81)

In the tales, Hicks seems to be reliving his own experiences. His telling statement about the wind blowing through Jack's house, "like I've had it here," refers to his own youthful battle with the cold. He adds to the traditional narrative his own personal touch. As Isbell explains, "[Hicks] has known cold, has known hunger. Such a story is best told by one who has lived it" (81).

In the tale, Jack decides to stop the northwest wind from blowing by stuffing his cap in the hole where it comes out. This technique of stopping wind has a personal slant for Hicks; he explains to Smith that he had stuffed his pants in a hole one night. A chunk of the wall fell out "right where my head was a-layin'…[and] snow was a-pepperin' in on my face, and I knew I wouldn't live 'til mornin'" (5).

Although Jack sets out on a quest for the northwest wind, he is stopped by a magical stranger who gives him a tablecloth that will always provide food. Jack agrees to return home with his magical bounty, but, while on the road, three brothers rob him. Jack returns to the magical stranger's house and is given a hen that lays golden eggs. Once again he agrees to abandon his quest and return home, but the brothers steal his chicken. Jack makes his way back to the magical stranger's house and is given a club that will beat anything on command. The three brothers try to take the club, but Jack uses it to force them to return the magical tablecloth and the hen that lays the gold eggs (Isbell 81-84).

When Jack employs the club to attack the three brothers, he merely acts with grim realism in a world in which passiveness seems impossible. The greed of the three brothers makes them overstep their bounds; if they had not bothered Jack for a third time, he would have passed by their house without retaliation for the first two thefts. The final theft is more problematic—the attempted villainy by the brothers leads to their undoing. Jack is unwilling to let them steal everything and leave his family destitute; he has to find the proper place to draw the line and stand up for his rights. This is the lesson that Hicks draws from his own life. "Everyone's out to hold up fer himself, but not go for cheatin. There ain't nobody goin to hold up fer ye. That's what hurt me so bad and made me suffer as a kid. I didn't know to hold up fer myself" (McDermitt 7).

Jack's acquisition of the magical implements provides his family with all of the necessities for life on Beech Mountain—food, money, and wood to burn. The tale may begin in the cold and the hunger associated with the mountain families of Appalachia, but it ends with the statement, "Jack and his mama lived on easy, whatever time they lived after that" (Isbell 84). Hicks seems to find comfort in knowing that such material success exists, if only in myth.

Along with incorporating his own life history into the Jack Tales, Hicks will occasionally use his personal experiences to highlight meaning within the narratives. For example, in an interview with Joseph Daniel Sobol for *The Storyteller's Journey*, Doug Lipman relates a storytelling experience he had with Hicks. When a listener asks about his childhood, Hicks explains about having to run the farm. One day it is too much for him, so he decides to run away. He climbs to the top of the hill for his last view of home. There, he thinks about his mother, who is physically ill, and walks back to the farm (114).

Immediately after telling this personal narrative, Hicks launches into the story of "Hardy Hard-Head" or "Hardy Hard-Ass" (transcribed by Sobol in "Jack in the Raw"). In this version, Jack is on a quest for a wife. He follows a path in the woods until it diverges at an oak tree. Not knowing the proper direction, Jack stops and invites the old man sitting under the tree to share his meal. After this interlude, Hicks includes a passage unique to his version of the tale:

> Well, as he got full, all he could eat, he said, "Young man, I know where you've a-goin'."
> An' said, "You're all the man 't's ever treated me right, that's come by here."
> Said, "All the others has sassed me.
> Said they wasn't gonna give nothin' to eat to a thing like me."
> An' he said, "Up in there is a b'ilin' spring."
> An' he hewed out a stick, An' he said, "If you've got faith, I can help ye."
> An' he hewed the stick out, re'ch it to Jack, an' said, "If you can turn that spring to wine, you've got faith."
> Said, "Take this stick up there an' stir in it."
> An' Jack got up there—just him, is all he seed there—an' he stirred an' stirred.
> His arm—changed hands, his arm was a-givin' out an' he says, "Bedads."
> He says, "Don't seem like I've got much faith."
> About that time, he thought it looked a little pink, an' that just made it turn to wine that quick.
> Then when it turned, there stood the man.
> Said, "Gawd Give!
> You've got faith, Son—Young Man." (Sobol 17-18)

By combining the two stories, Hicks draws attention to the inherent allegory in the narratives. Both his own moment on the hill and Jack's interlude on the path become metaphorically charged vehicles for presenting the quest for faith.

In listening to stories with allegorical elements, one needs to begin with the literal story—the plot—and attend to the action as carefully as possible. During this process the allegorical dimensions gradually begin to appear in the narrative. For instance, both tales present characters so entwined with their environments that images of place embody the characters' state of mind. Hicks instills himself at the top of a hill—the furthest point he can reach and still maintain contact with his family: One more step will launch him into unknown territory and sever him from all family and community ties. Hicks places Jack at a literal crossroads in the forest with no idea of the correct path to follow [eventually revealed as through the air]. By almost losing their physical orientation, both characters illustrate to the listeners what it feels like to be on the brink of losing one's ethical bearings as well.

Hicks translates the complexities of ethical situations into physical ones, but it is crucial when listening to the narratives never to simply discard the literal level. Rather, the allegorical elements compliment the literal narrative, giving it a greater depth of meaning. For example, the journey Hicks takes away from his family is ultimately internal, and the audience members learn much about his character as he regains a deeper purpose in life by coming to know himself and by committing his efforts toward his family's survival. It is a story about his attempt to rise above his private miseries and to become once more a contributing member of his community. Yet the tale ends and does not present a record of his achievements. The Jack Tale that immediately follows his narration must carry that burden.

By telling "Hardy Hard-Head" or "Hardy Hard-Ass" after his own life story, Hicks emphasizes the intertwining relationship between the narratives. Jack's story also presents a conversion—a turning from a level of weak faith to a strong and powerful faith that changes water into wine. Yet for all the religious implications this act could engender, the tale is about having faith in one's own abilities and good nature; it is not centered solely on Jack's religious growth, but on his total personal growth and what he achieves from choosing the correct path—a magical air ship, good friends, and a wife. Jack's subsequent life all boils down to that one particular moment and that one particular decision to assert the faith in himself.

The allegorical dimension also generalizes Jack's experience; it makes his encounter at the stream a striking image of a situation that could happen to any person. In listening to such an allegory one shifts continually between apprehending the character as an individual caught up in a particular situation—using faith to change water into wine—and viewing him as a representation of what any person could experience in the same type of situation—changing his life by having faith in his own abilities and nature.

The combination of the two tales also presents an opportunity to explore the initiation rites inherent in the stories. In the *Theory and History of Folklore*, Propp states his belief that folktales were originally an intricate part of ritual and initiation rites. Overtime this connection was severed as religious belief in the efficacy of the rite decreased. The tales continued in an independent form while still referencing certain tribal elements, such as exile, going into the forest, a journey, a stay in another realm, and a return from the other realm after gaining certain practical and ritual knowledge (Propp 64-73, 469-470). According to Propp, the tales are not actively operating in modern society; they are a collection of vestiges from a prior era.

In Hicks's narrative we can see that the form of initiation is still operative. His journey into the forest is not merely a collection of vestiges, but a narrative description of his own life experience. Upset by the conditions at home, Hicks travels into the wilderness. He stays in isolation until he gains perspective on his life, and then returns home. These actions correspond to Propp's elements and are carried through to "Hardy Hard-Head" or "Hardy Hard-Ass" as Hicks emphasizes the intertwining relationship between the two narratives. Jack's fictional journey is provided with a sense of immediacy from the connection to Hicks's personal experience.

Hicks juggles the two narratives and endows the comparatively simple stories with extraordinary resonance. The allegorical dimensions have a complex effect on the characters. Indeed, Hicks's own relation to Jack is complex, as always when he turns autobiography into fiction. In *The Storytellers' Journey*, Spalding Gray, a storyteller from New York, remarks that Hicks "is a genuine autobiographical storyteller. He's speaking from the first person, he is also enjoying his stories, he's both in and out of them" (Sobol 113).

Throughout his life Hicks has incorporated the store of general knowledge found in the Jack Tales into his own individual situation. He places his own experiences within the tales and allows his listeners to move beyond the general confines of their own lives and perhaps extend the scope of their own knowledge.

3

The Form of Oral Storytelling

Perhaps the simplest definition of mankind is that he is the storytelling animal.

—Piers Anthony

People in the United States live more or less in surrender to stories which center on their own lives, the lives of others, and/or the lives that follow fictional forms. Even those who deliberately reject the aspects of modern society which project an imagined reality—magazines, novels, television programs, and movies—must still conduct their lives within the realm of story. The anecdotes of daily life they share with loved ones, the reports they must deliver at work, and the jokes they share with friends all contain a certain narrative quality. Such narratives, as Robert Scholes and Robert Kellogg explain in *The Nature of Narrative*, possess two defining characteristics: a storyteller and a story (4). Oral art forms also require a third characteristic: a listener. Oral storytelling is based on the idea that an oral relationship exists between the tellers and the listeners. Within this relationship, storytellers construct a narrative which in turn is influenced by audience response. The audience members are participants rather than observers and help to shape not only the behavior of the storyteller, but also the structure of the tale.

In this chapter, I will initially focus on scholarly and critical concepts of the nature of orality in narrative and then summarize its significance in the folktale.

THE ELEMENTS OF STORIES

In *Telling the American Story*, Livia Polanyi identifies three elements that must be present in order for a storyteller to create a story. First, a teller must "encode a specific past time narrative description" of events and circumstances within a certain time frame (33). That is, it is a formal feature of narratives that events occur in the past and be spread out in time. In "The Transformation of Experience in Narrative Syntax," William Labov explains in linguistic terms that storytellers recapitulate past events and experiences for their listeners by "matching a verbal sequence of clauses to [a] sequence of events" the listeners inferred "actually occurred" (359-360). Because the teller's act of telling a story creates for listeners a natural association between the discourse and the experience, the storyteller's words create a perception of time, place, and events that can become "real" for the listeners. This ingrained universe in miniature (what Polanyi terms a "story-world") includes all relevant aspects of nature, mankind, the works of mankind, and the supernatural (Polanyi 33).

Second, Polanyi believes that there must be a reason for a story to be told. The teller is in search of a way to reveal the meaning of his or her narrative to the audience. A story describes a series of actions taken or experiences undergone by characters who are shown either changing situations or reacting to changes with a continuity of subject matter sufficient to make the chronological sequence significant. This process of transforming the storyworld through manipulation of action and key experiences allows the narrator an opportunity to reveal meaning (33).

Third, Polanyi adds the art of presentation. A story must be structured artfully so that audiences can identify its most salient details (33). This process centers around what Deborah Tannen refers to as "involvement strategies"—ways in which storytellers signify importance to their listeners (17). Involvement strategies are evaluative. They present information in ways that shape a hearer's perceptions (29). Those ways, beside the use of narrative, include: tropes; rhythm; dialogue; indirectness; imagery and detail; figures of speech; and repetition and variation of certain words or parts of speech (17).

Many elements Polanyi associates with "story" can be clearly identified in "Hardy Hard-Head," a traditional tale adapted by Ed Stivender, a storyteller whose repertoire includes both life-experience stories and Jack Tales. Stivender creates a past time narrative with a description of specific events and circumstances, incorporates specific involvement strategies, such as the use of imagery and detail, rhythm and repetition, and figures of speech, and utilizes both rhythm and dialogue to stress salient events in the narrative that reveal meaning to the audience. Stivender's narrative revolves around the life of a young man named Jack. Being the third born child, Jack is not well regarded and often suffers emotional and physical privations at the hands of his family. He leaves the somewhat tenuous security of his home in order to rescue an imprisoned princess and learns

36   Ray Hicks and the Jack Tales

that to deal with all the challenges life has to offer he does need friends. Stivender begins this way:

> One morning Jack and his brother Will and his brother Tom were sitting around the breakfast table.
> Jack said, "pass the milk please." And he passed the milk to Jack. He looked on the side of the milk carton. There was a picture of a young girl with a crown on her head. Above the picture it said, "Missing Princess." Below the picture it said, "Princess has been kidnapped by an Evil Wizard, cast under a spell, taken into the woods. One thousand dollar reward for anyone that can find the princess and break the spell." Then there was a toll-free "1-800" number on the back. ("Hardy Hard-Head")

Though Stivender plays ironically with the historical frame of the narrative when he places the picture of the missing princess with the crown on a milk carton, he eventually returns to the practice of traditional narrative. To create the story-world, he includes at the very outset those aspects of human existence typically addressed in traditional stories: life and death, threat and reward, innocence and villainy. But, in addition, he mixes the humbler spheres of the home and the community with that of the supernatural. Beginning with such traditional themes and settings, as Labov suggests of storytelling in general, allows a teller to orient his listeners to the time, place, and conditions of persons included in the narrative (364).

To introduce the broader elements of existence in a traditional way, Stivender simplifies imagery and details. Each item—the breakfast table, the milk carton, and the Princess's crown—is meant to create a generic imaged to be made personal by the audience. Such simplicity, Tannen explains, allows a teller to convey unstated meaning (23). For example, while it would be difficult to believe that every listener would envision exactly the same type of breakfast table—differences could include size, materials, color, design, and so forth—the basic, generic, idea of "table" would remain and still serve the storyteller's purpose. As Polanyi reveals, storytellers use such limited descriptions largely to reinforce the world view they share with their audiences (13). "The narrator relies upon [a] common understanding," Polanyi remarks, to encode thematic messages and to create clarity (13). In this situation, because Stivender assumes he shares beliefs and values with his audience, he can use a verbal "shorthand" to make his assumptions clear.

The most important aspect of Jack's journey to the Wizard's castle is that he make friends who will help him in his time of need. To focus the audience's attention on the salient events of the narrative, Stivender establishes a rhythmic form. He starts with a simple phrase:

> "Say, fellow. What's your name?"
> "My name is Hardy Hard-Head. What's yours?"
> "My name's Jack. Want to come on my boat?"
> "I'd love to."
> Hardy Hard-Head got on the boat and they took it up and up and up and up. ("Hardy Hard-Head")

Stivender begins successive sentences with the same group of words to establish one form of what Tannen refers to as "figures of speech":

> Jack yelled down, "hey, fellow. What's your name?"
> "My name is Drinkwell. What's yours?"
> "My name is Jack. Want to come on my boat?"
> "I'd love to."
> So Drinkwell got on the boat and they took it up and up and up. ("Hardy Hard-Head")

In order to stress the idea that Jack must gather many friends (or friendly people) around him before he faces the Wizard, Stivender incorporates more than one speaker into the rhythmic, formulaic, phrases and allows exchange between them. The dialogue is intended to heighten the audience's awareness of the event. As Jack invites people to travel on his magical airship, he learns, in the process, of each passenger's special ability:

> Jack yelled down, "hey, fellow. What's your name?"
> "My name is Eatwell. What's yours?"
> "Mine's Jack. Wanta come on my boat?"
> "I'd love to."
> So Eatwell got on the boat and they took it up and up and up. ("Hardy Hard-Head")

Even as the repetition of the phrasing calls attention to itself as a pattern, it also creates an expectation of more of the same—and, indeed, Jack picks up other passengers named Hearwell, Seewell, Smellwell, and Shootwell. By using the formulaic phrasing throughout the story, Stivender develops a rhythm and a series of orderly changes and variations. When he deliberately breaks from this pattern, he forces the audience to recognize the variation and focus on the significance of the

38   Ray Hicks and the Jack Tales

new. For instance, when Stivender breaks the pattern to introduce "Runwell," he enables the girl to mention the thematic word "friends":

> Jack yells down, "hey, young woman, what's your name?"
> "My name's Judy. But my friends on the track team call me Runwell. What's yours?"
> "Mine's Jack. Wanta come on my boat?"
> "I'd love to." So Runwell got on the boat and they took it up and up and up and up and up. (my emphasis).

It is important that Stivender establish Jack's relationship to the other travelers quickly. The story centers around the theme of friendship in general and, specifically, on how friends use their natural talents to help one another through difficulties. By breaking the rhythm and inserting the name "Judy," Stivender is able to draw attention to the next part of the passage, "but my friends...call me Runwell." Stivender is able to establish that Jack and the rest of the airship passengers are friends because they address Judy by the name of Runwell. Therefore, little narrative time passes before the audience understands that the "friends" must or will work together cohesively as a team to rescue the princess.

Stivender also reinforces the importance of community through the theme of friendship. Although he has traveled away from his home, he is still connected to a society of friendly people. In fact, Jack cannot effectively function as a hero on his own. He needs the support of the others in his new community to rescue the princess.

Stivender uses repetition and variation as the means to show the progression of experience and action that is so important in a temporal art form. When a repeated word or phrase becomes unmistakably evident and imposes itself upon the consciousness of listeners, particularly from the beginning of the story, it obviously affects their subsequent perceptions. In the case of "Hardy Hard-Head," Stivender imposes form on Jack's world by the use of rhythmically repeated phrases. Since Stivender beats out the rhythm so insistently through repetition, he mesmerizes his audience while at the same he enables it to focus on the variations that emerge clearly within the repetitions. The pattern of repetition and variation provides clues to the orderly and discernible changes that affect meaning.

A story's meaning depends upon which involvement strategies are both emphasized by the teller and embraced by the audience. A storyteller can juggle involvement strategies constantly and utilize more than one simultaneously. Since stories may have many involvement strategies, it is still possible for listeners in the same audience to focus on different aspects. "Hardy Hard-Head," for instance, can be interpreted as a story about a young man's journey toward adulthood, about the importance of being kind to strangers, or about the necessity of friendship during difficult times. Ideally, a storyteller will create his or her narrative to unify all of the story elements, including the involvement strategies, so that the story will not carry the danger of reduction of meaning—the audience will understand such interpretations as those above and more. The elements of a story are meant to function collectively and the teller must provide the means for audiences to comprehend how they fit together in order to grant a narrative its due complexity.

MORPHOLOGY OF FOLKTALES

In *Structuralism in Literature*, Scholes focuses on the idea of a self-regulating system of narrative "that adapts to new conditions by transforming its features while retaining its systematic structure" (10). He explains that texts are systems in which literary units must relate to one another to generate meaning (10). There are set conditions under which a storyteller makes a story and a narrative grammar whose rules specify the organizational structure of the literary units within a tale. Storytellers need to learn the syntactical conventions in order to obtain the competence to generate the stories of their culture. In *Image, Music, Text* Roland Barthes explains that the storytellers who best master the conventions are the most esteemed by their listeners (114-115).

In the *Morphology of the Folktale*, Propp explores the common form of folktales and creates a paradigm for dealing with how literary units (in this case characters and their actions) interact with each other and generate meaning. Although devoted to analyzing a collection of Russian folktales, Propp's study offers important insights for those interested in oral narrative because his observations have wide applicability to folktales of all nations. Indeed, he seems to have discovered some of the basic functions found in all narratives. Most narratives contain certain characters, such as heroes, villains, and donors, and they perform certain actions, such as rescue a Prince/Princess, fight in direct combat, or offer advice. Propp demonstrates that there is a universal structure at the level of the narrative itself and not merely at the level of themes or motifs. There is a logic to narratives and they are constructed according to rules that have not varied greatly over the centuries.

Propp elicits thirty-one different forms of "functions" that he describes as "an act of character, defined from the point of view of its significance for the course of the action" (21). The functions are the building blocks out of which narratives are constructed and represent an action by one character and a reaction or counter-action by an opposing character. Such functions are stable, limited in number, and independent of the personage by which they are fulfilled. The actions taken by the characters, such as flight, interdiction, or interrogation, reveal their meaning in part from their placement in the course of the narrative (Propp 21). Thus Function I in Propp's system, in which "one of the members of a family absents himself from home," is defined both by the absence and the fact that it occurs at the beginning of the tale (26). An absence occurring at the end of the narrative would not be classified as Function I. The absence of the family member is not defined by nature. The action is paramount and the circumstantial details play no part in the function. Propp focuses on the basic action and tends to ignore the circumstantial details.

Propp believes folktales include a maximum number of functions that succeed each other in the same order (21-22). Not all functions, however, are present in all tales, so the structure that Propp postulates only partially manifests in any particular tale.

Propp's functions can be applied to the Appalachian Jack Tales successfully, often with relatively little adaptation. However, several of the characters in Ray Hicks's version of "Jack and the Bean Tree" do not fit within Propp's paradigm and create an interesting quandary: what function do the characters fill in the organizational structure of the narrative?

Hicks begins his narrative:

> Jack and his mother they stayed years ago in their log cabin and it come and the father deceased. Just them and a livin' to get.
> So they had one milk cow and finally they got down to starvation and [Jack's mother] said, "Jack, my boy, we're gonna probably have to sell our milk cow. Which," she says, "I hate to sell." Said, "you take it…take the cow."
> Said, "don't you take no less than fifty guineas for it."
> And so Jack put the rope on and took off and he come along. Gone and met up with a man sellin' magic beans.
> [The magic bean seller] said, "now this ain't a normal bean. [It is] a magic bean."
> And so the man took the cow and Jack took the bean and carried it back. ("Jack and the Bean Tree")

When Jack returns with the magic bean, his mother demonstrates her disappointment by beating the boy and throwing the bean out the window.

It is at this point that there is a sharp division of the narrative. The exchange of the bean for the cow is what Barthes terms a "cardinal function." He believes that functions do not all constitute the same level of importance in a narrative. Unlike catalyzer functions, cardinal functions modify the nature of the story (94). For a function to be considered "cardinal," it must directly affect the subsequent development of the story (Barthes 93-94). The action between Jack and the magic bean seller falls within the "cardinal" category because, if the action is never completed (and the bean is never acquired), then, as Barthes explains, the linear progression of the story would change dramatically and the narrative would progress along a different path (94). The first character that needs to be defined in Hicks's tale is that of the hero. Propp separates "heroes" into two distinct categories; victim heroes who suffer directly from the actions of the villain and seeker heroes who alleviate the suffering or misfortunes of others (36-38). Yet, as will be demonstrated, Jack does not completely fit into either of these categories. He is victimized only once (at the beginning of the narrative) and his subsequent actions (after he climbs the bean tree and kills the giants) cause rather than alleviate suffering.

In the beginning of the tale a number of Propp's functions can be found that seem to place Jack in the role of a victim hero. As previously discussed, Propp's Function I deals with a member of the family who is absent from home (26). The death of Jack's father is an extreme form of this absence and Jack and his mother are left to fend for themselves. When Jack's mother warns the boy not to sell the cow for less than fifty guineas, she is fulfilling Propp's Function II in which "an interdiction is addressed to the hero" (26).

Jack violates the interdiction (fulfilling Propp's Function III) by selling the cow for a magic bean rather than money. "At this point," Propp explains, "a new personage, who can be termed the villain, enters the tale. His role is to disturb the peace of a happy family" (27). Because Propp believes that characters reveal their meaning in part from their placement in the course of the narrative, the next character to be introduced should be a villain (21). If this structure is followed, then the character of the magic bean seller in Hicks's adaptation should follow the actions designated for a villain. He begins by disturbing the peace within Jack's family; when Jack returns home, his mother cries,"magic bean? We can't live that way!" She throws the bean out the window and beats Jack for his failure. The peace within the family is definitely broken.

Yet the magic bean seller does not follow the other Functions designated for the villain by Propp. For example, he does not conform to Functions IV and V and make an attempt at reconnaissance or discern information about his victim (Propp 28-29). In fact, after the exchange of the bean for the cow, the magic bean seller disappears from the narrative.

The other option for the character of the magic bean seller is that of donor of a magical agent or help. Because of the magic bean seller's placement in the narrative, this would shift Jack's character into that of a seeker hero. The basic actions in the beginning also seem to follow Propp's structure for the seeker hero: Lack (Function VIIIa), dispatch of the hero (Function IX), and departure (Function XII) (35-39). The next character to be introduced should be a donor who offers for exchange a magical agent to the hero (Function XII, subsection ten) (42). But this designation for the magic bean seller is also filled with difficulties. As Propp explains, one of the most crucial aspects in the relationship between the donor and the hero is their initial encounter where the hero is tested in some way, often by being given the opportunity of feeding the future donor or of saving the donor's life (34-42). Jack is never tested by the magic bean seller and his quality of character is never established.

There are rare instances when the seeker hero may purchase a magic agent "without the slightest preparation" (Propp 46). If the transaction is placed in this category, then another problem arises with the designation of the magic bean seller as a donor. Propp explains that "it is always possible to be governed by the principle of defining a function according to its consequences" (67). If the magic bean seller is a donor, then why do his actions cause harm (in the form of a beating) to the hero? The donor figure would be assuming the actions of a villain by disrupting the family dynamic between the hero and his mother.

In the *Course in General Linguistics*, Ferdinand de Saussure posits the idea that relationships between textual units are important in generating meaning. He establishes that concepts "are purely differential" and derive their meanings "not from their positive content" but from their relationship to other terms in the system (117). "The most precise characteristics" of concepts, he adds, are "in being what others are not" (Saussure 117). Saussure's insight about the meaning of concepts being based on a relationship of opposition to other concepts can be applied to characters and actions. Binary opposition is fundamental to the production of meaning. Patterns are found among characters and actions. The characters in narratives (and their actions) have meaning because of the figures who oppose them (and oppose their actions).

Part of the problem with finding a designation for the character of Jack at the beginning of the narrative lies in the fact that there is no established polar opposite for his character at the syntactic level of the narrative; he cannot be definitively characterized either as a seeker or a victim at this point because his relationship with magic bean seller remains undefined.

After the exchange between Jack and the magic bean seller, there is a sharp division in the character of the hero. At this point in the narrative, Jack's character moves away from the category of the victim hero and closely resembles the seeker hero.

After the bean is thrown out the window, Hicks continues, it sprouts and the plant eventually grows taller than the house. Jack climbs the bean tree three times. On his first trip he finds a house as big as a mountain and a friendly lady giant. She protects Jack from her man-eating giant husband by hiding him in an old oven. The giant thinks he smells an intruder and wants to search him out, but his wife convinces him that he is merely smelling the evening meal. After the giant falls asleep, Jack steals his knife. The second time Jack climbs the bean tree, the giant lady hides him in a pat of butter until her husband falls asleep. Jack then steals the giant's gun. During his last trip up the bean tree, the giant lady hides Jack under her apron. After both giants fall asleep, Jack steals their bedspread. The noise of this wakens the giant and he goes after Jack, but the boy reaches the ground first and chops down the bean tree. Jack finds both giants dead from the fall. He does not think much about the giant husband, but he cries over the giant lady's corpse ("Jack and the Bean Tree).

Jack's journey up the bean tree corresponds with Propp's Function XV, subsection five, where the hero is transformed to an object of search through the use of a stationary means of communication (50-51). By climbing the bean tree (magical agent), Jack locates the giant lady (magical helper) who protects him from the giant (villain). The giant is revealed to be a murderous cannibal who eventually attempts to kill Jack and pursues him down the bean tree (Function XXI). Jack saves himself from this pursuit by chopping down the bean tree (Function XXII) and killing the giant (Function XXX).

Although Hicks's narrative follows many of Propp's functions of the seeker hero, Jack does not begin his journey to alleviate the suffering or misfortunes of others. Function XIX, in which the initial lack is liquidated through the actions of the hero, is never fulfilled (Propp 53). Neither the cow nor the fifty guineas are recovered. Jack steals a knife, a gun, and a bell-covered bedspread from the giant for himself. He treats these items as playthings and never attempts to replace his mother's property.

Propp's *Morphology of the Folktale* shows that narratives have a certain definite form and a certain logic underlying that form. When applied to most Appalachian Jack Tales, Propp's functions serve to define the general structure of the oral narratives. Yet these functions are not all inclusive; tales like Hicks's version of "Jack and the Bean Tree" do not completely fit within Propp's paradigm. In part, this is because oral narrative is an evolving form and every storyteller is part of that evolution. Functions will be added or eliminated and new categories of characters will emerge. Even in a literate society where many oral narratives are committed to print (and thus exist in a permanent form within the culture), adaptation still endures.

ORAL ART FORM IN A LITERATE SOCIETY

Piers Anthony suggests that mankind can be defined as "the storytelling animal." In today's mainstream American society, lives are filled with stories—but they occur mainly in books, television, and movies. The oral traditional has been devalued in a culture that has access to instantaneous multi-media entertainment. Yet the practice of oral storytelling in America continues.

What does it mean to practice an "oral" tradition in a culture whose definitions of "literature" typically encompass only the written word? If the printed page is the primary "literary" image offered within a culture, how does such imagery influence the way in which an audience receives an oral art form? If an oral story, for example, is recorded in printed form, how does the process of writing affect the storyteller's voice, either in perception or in fact? Should the storyteller try to blend his narrative into a literary mold, removing all traces of orality? Would such a project even be feasible? These are questions fundamental to the study of the American oral tradition.

It is true, of course, that in order to provide any type of answer for these questions, we must avoid the ambiguity of the term "oral" as it is understood in a literate society. In particular, we must focus on how the process of oral composition differs from that of oral recitation. Within a literate culture, the term "oral" most commonly refers merely to words spoken rather than written; if we extend the term to include the art of oral narrative, however, any definition of "oral" becomes more problematic. Indeed, the problem is more than a matter of definition—it lies in the mind-set of the culture itself.

ORAL COMPOSITION

As Saussure explains, the members of a literate culture think of writing as the basic form of language and project the categories and processes of literate thought onto non-literate works and cultures (23-24). Saussure believes that it is important for members of a literate society to recognize that oral speech underpins all communications and that writing merely re-presents the spoken word (23-24). Whereas language exists, and has existed, in many cultures without a written form, writing cannot exist without a prior oral form.

What is less immediately obvious is the extent to which a literate mind-set animates the functioning of analytic thought. In *Orality and Literacy: The Technologizing of the Word*, Ong explains that writing not only enlarges the potentiality of language, but restructures human thought processes (7-8). Extended sequential analysis occurs within a culture only after its members interiorize writing. Until, as Ong relates, an exterior system for storing knowledge exists, the only possible way to process and retain information is within the human mind (9-12).

Within a primary oral culture, before the knowledge of writing exists, thought processes do not adhere to a strict linear pattern; rather, they are structured to fit into formulas that increase the mind's ability to recall information. In *The Making of Homeric Verse*, Milman Parry defines the oral formula as "a group of words which is regularly employed under the same metrical conditions to express a given essential idea" (272). By analyzing *The Iliad* and *The Odyssey*, Parry theorized that the formulas were the creations of many generations of bards who worked within a poetic tradition. Poets who used these formulas were able to make verses extemporaneously without having to depend upon the technique of verbatim memorization.

Given their prominence within a primary oral culture, it is not surprising to find the same types of formulas within the current oral tradition, even though most storytellers in the United States are literate. In her study of Xhosa poets, Ruth Finnegan discovered that oral formulaic thought and expression do not vanish as soon as one takes a pen in hand (70). The tradition continues to exist as long as there are people willing to learn the processes and preserve the techniques.

Within any form of oral art, there will be a predominance of formulas, but, to a lesser extent, formulas also appear in written texts. In *The Singer of Tales*, Albert B. Lord argues that "the presence of [some] 'formulas' in 'literary' style indicates its origin in oral style. [Such] formulas are vestigial" (130). In written texts, however, formulas often collapse into what the literate culture denigrates as "clichés"—words or phrases criticized for the very lack of originality that makes

46   Ray Hicks and the Jack Tales

them formulaic. Thus, to put it another way, if oral formulas, which survive only because they are set expressions that serve as mnemonic and structural aids, are required to submit to techniques of linear analysis and a literate culture's definition of "originality," then they operate from the first at a disadvantage. Inevitably, of course, formulas are also present in literary versions of oral stories, for a story's formulas from the oral tradition must play a prominent part in the formation of the written text. But there are other instances of formulaic language less obviously devalued from the oral tradition.

"Once upon a time there was…" is an example of an oral formula that has survived within the literate culture of the United States. Because it is so familiar, it is rarely used in printed texts and is primarily relegated to the genre of children's stories and fairy-tales. It creates a series of expectations within the listener by providing a formal tone to the event, establishing a non-linear form, ritualizing the narrative, and referencing the past through the process of repetition. A listener hears the formula "Once upon a time there was…" and realizes immediately that a story will follow.

What is interesting about this particular formula is its prominence in the current oral tradition. It appears in a great majority of storytellers' repertoires because, as Laura Simms explains, "the beginning of the story itself creates an imaginative landscape through which we [the audience] will travel" (8). A storyteller uses a formula like "Once upon a time there was…" to establish a connection with the audience and to create an atmosphere of reciprocity that does not and cannot exist on the printed page.

In a literate society, the use of formulas and formulaic elements within a text can help to determine whether a work is based in or influenced by the oral tradition. For example, comparing two versions of Maude Gentry Long's "Jack and the Heifer Hide,"—an oral märchen passed down through several generations of her family—reveals one difference between literate and oral dominance within a narrative. In 1937, Richard Chase used Long's tale as the major source for his Jack Tales version of "The Heifer Hide," and in 1955, Long recorded "Jack and the Heifer Hide" for the Library of Congress's Archive of Folk Music. The contrast between Chase's literary adaptation and Long's oral tale is quite marked, beginning with Chase's decision to reduce repetition and remove Jack's name from the title of the short story. Further variations can be seen in the opening sentences.

Chase writes:

Well, Jack's daddy had a tract of land back in the mountains and decided he'd give it to the boys to work. (161)

Long states:

Once upon a time there was a man who had three sons: Jack, Will, and Tom. (107)

Each version begins the story, but the style of the sentences and the techniques of imparting information reveal a difference between oral and literate dominance within a text. In his "Preface," Chase admits "in editing these stories we have taken the advice of our informants, and the publisher, and retold them, in part, for this business of getting them into print" (xi). He describes the literate culture's influence on "The Heifer Hide," recognizing that it is no longer a completely accurate representation of how Long told the tale, but, rather, that it utilizes (and therefore consciously expresses) a "print-enabled" word choice and structure.

Beyond the removal of the traditional opening formula, Chase's adaptation raises problems in relation to the literate culture's understanding of the structural basis of oral storytelling, and, in particular, produces questions concerning the necessity of repetitions within it. The literate representation of the oral text becomes troubling when entangled with the culture's desire for originality, and that desire leads the text of "The Heifer Hide" to be constructed following literate patterns of thought—if the names of "the boys" are not available within the current sentence, a reader can look back at the preceding pages or scan forward to acquire the missing details. No such reading technique is available for an oral art form. As Ong relates, no process exists by which to "look up" information. Indeed, within a primary oral culture, the term has no form of translation and is understood only when the concept of writing is introduced (31). "Without writing," Ong explains, "words as such have no visual presence, even when the objects they represent are visual" (31). Once the words are spoken, they have no tangible presence in the world and exist only in memory. Unless Long states the names "Jack, Will, and Tom" in her opening, the audience will miss a vital piece of information. In this instance, one can see the possible limitations of the oral transmission of the tale and how writing actually increases the probability of a full disclosure of information.

Long's original version of "Jack and the Heifer Hide" fits under the classification of "oral art form" as it is orally composed. But a verbatim recitation from

48   Ray Hicks and the Jack Tales

memory of "The Heifer Hide" is also oral, and so is reading Chase's text aloud; they are all spoken and heard. The processes of composition and recitation allow the tales to be received in the same manner, with the only variance thus far existing in the way the information is presented, by utilizing either formulas or non-formulaic elements.

Significantly, there is also a fundamental difference between oral composition and oral recitation within the element of performance. In an interview with Joseph Daniel Sobol for *The Storytellers' Journey*, Carol Birch discusses the contrast, focusing on her early training as a storyteller:

> I think [I was] trained in recitation—not in storytelling. It's a form of story-telling, but it's not telling.
> Because, I always liked literary tales.
> And people always said, "You can be more free with folktales, but you have to tell literary tales word for word." (40)

Within the technique of oral recitation, the desire for continuity is emphasized: all original thought lies with the author of the written text. Birch is instructed to tell her stories "word for word," but recognizes that this is different from "storytelling" and there is no room for her own innovations. To achieve this crucial difference—to place the ability to create in the hands of the performer—oral composition of any art form, whether storytelling or epic poetry, requires another element—composition in performance.

COMPOSITION IN PERFORMANCE

In *Oral Poetry: Its Nature, Significance, and Social Context* Finnegan explains that "there are…ways in which oral literature clearly does differ from written literature—chiefly…in the matter of its being performed" (137). In differentiating between the two forms of literature, she places at the forefront the significance of the performance—and also stresses that composition and performance are in varying degrees aspects of one process (137).

Utilizing Finnegan's criteria allows one to partially define storytelling as a public art form pre-supposing an audience and a performance. Simms reinforces this idea, describing storytelling as "a living art which takes place in the present between people" (9). This art is based on the idea that an oral relationship exists between the tellers and the listeners. Within the bounds of this relationship, the storyteller constructs both his/her "performing self" and a community of shared thought which in turn is influenced by audience response. Significantly, then, the audience members are participants rather than observers and help to shape not only the behavior of the storyteller, but also the structure of the tale—the words, the events, the tone, and even the plot.

To some degree, of course, all men, women, and children shape their behavior (particularly in public) in accordance with their awareness of the people in the immediate environment; this is part of what it means to be integrated with a society and a culture. In modern dramatic performances, this dimension of behavior often goes unexplored, since actors and audiences take it for granted, overlook it, or simply ignore it. Most storytellers have probed it, however, paying special attention to the capacity of human beings to reinvent their personalities in accordance with changing circumstances. In "Inside the Oral Medium," Donald Davis writes:

> In order to operate inside the oral medium, hearers are absolutely required, and the storyteller must be in dialogue with them.
> In such a dialogue, a teller's perceptive skills go to work and guide the tellings so that for this audience, in this time and place, the story being told is uniquely theirs. When storytellers are fully in the oral medium as coparticipants with their hearers, they edit, correct, lengthen, shorten, change, and add—all in the process of the storytelling event. (7)

Davis's description of the oral medium reveals how he attempts to ease the dialogue across the conversational chasm which exists between a storyteller and an audience. Audience members pick up a strand of the narrative, recognize its relevance to their lives, formulate their emotional response, and search the teller's behavior and speech for a sign of mutual recognition. The audience response, as Polanyi notes, is necessarily limited. The members can indicate acceptance and understanding, but are not free in the public arena to continue the dialogue (32). Davis emphasizes that it is the storytellers' responsibility to "edit, correct, lengthen, shorten, change, and add" in order to create a feeling of a shared event between themselves and the listeners—a community type of bond—which enables every participant to grasp and evaluate the storytelling experience in the most comprehensive manner possible (7).

In "Jack and the Robbers," Ed Stivender begins by using first-person discourse to comment on the action and signal to his audience that he is the presiding spirit of the narrative. As Labov notes, Stivender is translating Jack's personal experience into dramatic form (396). All stories posit a particular relationship between the characters and the audience. In every case, it is the teller who determines what

50   Ray Hicks and the Jack Tales

kind of relationship this will be and how it will be accomplished through narrative mechanisms. When Stivender states, "my name's Jack, and I'd like to tell you a story about the time I went out to seek my fortune," he is using first-person discourse as an overt signature that proclaims his control over the narrative and the world that it constructs (68). This gives him a unique position and allows him to shift his voice into a first-person stance—although it is clearly not his story. In effect, Stivender introduces himself to the audience as Jack.

After the orientation, Stivender utilizes the techniques of characterization and dialogue. Rather than appearing as an omniscient narrator, he attempts to become each character, changing his posture, vocal timbre, and choice of language as appropriate:

> I said to my mama, "I'm going out to seek my fortune."
> She said, "You be careful, Jack. Don't talk to any strangers on the road."
> I replied, "Don't worry about me, Mama.
> I'll be all right."
> So I went down the road to seek my fortune. (68)

As Polanyi explains, the audience can recognize that Stivender is not really two, or three, or four different people, but his performance allows the members to suspend disbelief and enter the storyworld (33). The use of dialogue enhances this effect and the audience can watch the events as if they were transpiring upon the stage.

When narrating a story, Stivender is considered a performer—explicitly when he speaks to the audience in the first person; and implicitly as he manipulates the characters in his story, who act for both him and the audience as the tale unfolds.

In "Jack's Adventures in Toronto," Kay Stone describes the process of a shared storytelling event. Stone journeyed to the annual Toronto Storytelling Festival to interview Stewart Cameron and tape his "Jack and the Three Feathers," a traditional tale which involves a king and his three sons. Three boys between the ages of eight and eleven intruded upon Stone's taping. The storyteller acknowledged the boys and addressed parts of the story directly to them:

> "I am going to set you three lads a quest. Each one of you is to go off, where the winds will take you, and to come back with the most beautiful tablecloth in the entire world. And the one that comes back with the most beautiful, finely made tablecloth—that is the lad that will be the king after I go."
> [Here he turns and addresses the three boys as if he were the king, and to this they respond by giggling and pretending to take on the character of each

brother. They actually leave the room briefly and return, still laughing.] (Stone 258-259)

By locating the analysis of Cameron's storytelling at the interface between the audience, the performance, and the tale, one can begin to see the web of social relations between the participants given meaning without losing the integrity of the story. The form of the story becomes structurally significant as it matches the boys' personal experiences—as they pretend to "take on the character of each brother" (259). It is easy to recognize the shared cultural event when the audience participation—the boy's actions—is given expression and acknowledgment. The process of direct interaction between the teller and the audience yields a one-time site-specific interpretation of the story. Acknowledging the boys and their actions allows Cameron to leave the storyworld and step into the here and now—this moment, these children, and this performance.

Cameron's version of "Jack and the Three Feathers" is based on an adaptation by Jim Strickland. During Stone's recording, she relates how Strickland's arrival in the room mid-way through the tale causes Cameron to lose his concentration and to shift his language patterns from a casual conversational tone to a more formal and elaborate style (Stone 253).

Cameron tries to balance continuity (telling the story as he had heard it from Strickland) and interpretation (responding to his own performance craft and life experiences) when creating his own version of the tale (Stone 253). In a letter to Stone, Cameron writes:

> When I began telling [Jack and the Three Feathers] to my kids, I found that it changed considerably [according] to my audience's response. My son Duncan was heavily into the wonders of mud at the time and spent many hours mucking around in our "back garden." I naturally enlarged the importance of this part of the story[9] and Duncan became the role model for my Jack. (Stone 253-254)

In this instance Cameron reveals that his recorded version of "Jack and the Three Feathers" has been altered not only by the audience participation, but in the substance of the narrative before he even begins to speak. Cameron takes into account the context, the previous tellings, and the relationship between the teller and the audience, and explains how the story has been modified.

This capacity of the teller to adapt and transform his or her tale based on audience participation during each storytelling event may be represented as a dialogue between story and interpretation. Consider, first, that a story is always subject to interpretation. Stories begin as interpretation of experiences, events, natural phenomena, or cultural mores and taboos. Stories operate not simply in the realm of the mind as ideas, but to be convincing they also must have a basis in experience or social practice. Storytellers face the task of creating convincing tales for their audience without losing the integrity of the experiences. And once that story is formed and passed from one teller to the next, the same practice of interpretation can occur. This leads to a central question of composition in performance—if the narrative is adapted with each retelling, then how much adaptation can occur before the story is no longer acknowledged as being the same? In part, this is a question of perspective, for either continuity or discontinuity can be stressed; the practice of deliberate, conscious, narrative revision can be highlighted or downplayed. What seems reasonable, however, is the proposition that there will always be some built-in interpretations. Even in a traditional tale, such as "Jack and the Three Feathers," which has a high level of specialized organization, one can always find significant concentrations of interpretable material that a specific teller has "added" to satisfy his or her own performance craft.

PERFORMANCE CRAFT

Any performer of an art form imposes order upon the world by a process of calculated and informed selection. There are no accidents, for instance, in an oral story; every word, every line, every incident, and every character is the product of a shaping voice which knows its craft.

Within the process of oral recitation, the shaping voice belongs to the author of the printed text. All aspects of originality in word choice or form lie with the author. There is no lee-way for the oral performers' choices or innovations, unless they modify or adapt the text, in which case they will have drifted into the realm of oral composition. The very nature of print is to lock the words and phrases into one form, so that from the beginning to the end of a text's existence the same marks remain upon the page. Unless errors are made, each oral recitation will follow word-for-word and line-for-line the original text and provide an oral carbon-copy for the audience. In this sense it can be seen that oral recitation, whether occurring from verbatim memory or reading aloud, has little in common with the continuous narrative modification that takes place in oral composition.

Oral composition progresses one step beyond the process of oral recitation in the realm of creativity. As Lord explains, each traditional narrative begins with a set of themes which are not a "fixed set of words, but a grouping of ideas" regularly employed in the telling of a tale (68). Each story progresses from one group of themes to another to form a complete narrative. That this process is creative may at first seem surprising since, as W.F.H. Nicolaisen explains, "tradition seems to defy creativity and to exclude individuality" (123). However, the creative effort of each storyteller exists in maintaining the traditional elements of the tale while adapting the narrative to include their own innovations. Indeed, Lord stresses the fact that the experience of an oral narrator includes "nothing…to give him any idea that a theme can be expressed in only one set of words" (69).

One can explore a performer's interpretation within the process of oral composition by returning to the example of Long's "Jack and the Heifer Hide." This particular oral märchen has been passed from generation to generation in Long's Beech Mountain family and multiple versions are extant, including professional recordings by Long's cousins Marshall Ward and Hattie Presnell. The three interpretations of the tale follow the same overall theme of deception: Jack begins the cycle by selling his "magic" heifer hide to a gullible farmer, fools several other minor characters along the way, and ends by convincing his brothers to drown themselves in the river. The creative elements of oral composition—the application of each storyteller's performance craft—can be seen when comparing one segment of "Jack and the Heifer Hide" from each of the Beech Mountain storytellers.

All three tellers discuss the effects the sale of the "magic" cowhide has on Jack's life. After Jack reports the price his cowhide brought, his brothers kill all of their cows and attempt to sell the hides. His brothers are unsuccessful in their endeavor, so they decide to kill Jack and take his money. They tie Jack up in a sack and plan to throw him into the river. His brothers go out searching for rocks to add weight to the sack and leave Jack tied up at the side of the road. Jack has a conversation with a passing shepherd during which he convinces the older man to take his place by implying that whoever is in the sack is guaranteed to go to heaven. Before climbing into the sack, the shepherd gives Jack a flock of sheep.

The Beech Mountain storytellers follow the same pattern as each Jack character tricks the old shepherd into taking his place in the sack. The differences in the stories lie in the details. For example, Long uses two hundred thirty-two words to bring Jack's "conversation" alive (118-119). Presnell is more succinct at one hundred sixty-three words (Nicolaisen 143-144). Ward's version falls between Long and Presnell at two hundred and seven words (Nicolaisen 143).

Ward reveals himself as the most materialistic of the cousins, including not only three thousand sheep, but a dog, a fine horse, and a gold saddle in the deal between Jack and the shepherd (Nicolaisen 143). He uses seventy-five words to

54   Ray Hicks and the Jack Tales

describe the shepherd's possessions, as opposed to nine for Long and nineteen for Presnell. Presnell is at first vague with her "big bunch" of sheep, though she later refines it to a "thousand head" (Nicolaisen 143-144). Long does not seem concerned with the monetary gain that Jack will receive, only that the sheep are aesthetically pleasing (119).

Ward's materialism continues to be evident as the shepherd offers to swap his possessions for Jack's place in heaven. Ward's shepherd explains that "I got three thousand sheep, I got a fine horse, and I got a dog can take care of every one of these sheep. I tell you what I'll do. I'll swap places with you and give you all this," (Nicolaisen 143). This contrasts sharply with Long's shepherd, who uses a moral argument to urge Jack out of the sack. After Long's shepherd determines that Jack is indeed a young man, he insists that his advanced age gives him the right to go to heaven first: "Jack, I've wanted to go to heaven for so long! Listen, son, why you're just a boy! Get out of there, won't you please, and let me go in your place, and let me go to heaven?" (Long 119). Indeed, it appears that Long gives Jack the sheep almost as an afterthought by having the shepherd tell Jack to take the flock after the old man is tied up in the sack (119). Presnell falls between these two extremes, having the shepherd plead his case by pointing out the age difference between Jack and himself and then having him proffer the sheep as a bribe (Nicholaisen 144).

As Nicolaisen observes, every storyteller's adaptive use of detail helps to "make the story their own," but they never step beyond "the bounds within which tradition obliges them to operate" (148). Beyond their own interpretations, the storytellers express what they have inherited from the tradition by keeping the themes and the formulas[10] intact. Each retelling starts from within the tradition and then encompasses new conditions, but is still recognizable as being the same story.

Is the definition of mankind as "the storytelling animal" still relevant in a literate society? It is true that such a society embraces the printed page as the primary form of literature. It is true that storytellers within such a culture can consciously or unconsciously assimilate elements of literate thought processes into their own works. Indeed, it is also true that the literate cultural mind-set has affected the collection of oral art forms. But should these facts remove the term "storytelling" from the definition of mankind?

In Western society, literacy provides a way of preserving the essential lore of a culture, but the strength of storytelling in its current form lies in the participants' recognition that oral artists can move beyond the confines of the print medium and focus their works in oral composition, rather than oral recitation. Both the artist and the audience can affect the composition of a story during a performance, creating a shared event that is unique. And, although some adaptation and interpretation can occur, the storytellers continue to work within the bounds of tradition. Cumulatively, this effort reveals the oral artist's ability and desire to flourish. As long as there are people willing to learn the processes and preserve the techniques of the oral tradition, mankind can still be termed "the storytelling animal."

4

Passing the Torch: Ray Hicks's Influence on the Storytellers From Beech Mountain and Beyond

"When I'm watching Uncle Ray tell a tale, I get hypnotized. He becomes Jack when he's telling. And when I watch him, we both become Jack.

—Frank Proffitt Jr.

Interaction between storyteller and listeners helps to reinforce the particular events and history that shape people's lives and bind a culture together through the unique quality of human imagination. In *The Interpretation of Cultures*, Clifford Geertz argues that imagination is a social act and takes place in the public world. Imagination, Geertz suggests, is located in significant symbols—experience, images, and sounds—upon which humans have impressed meaning (362). It is through the cultural patterns these significant symbols generate that humans make sense of the events through which they live (363). By creating a product that stimulates the imagination through these significant symbols, oral artists who share aspects of their lives create a spontaneous relationship with members of a community.

As discussed in the second chapter, Ray Hicks is an expert at telling Jack Tales that reflect the regional folklore of Appalachia. The tales draw the audiences to them because, deriving from Hicks's heritage, they seem to share in his expression of communal history. "Not many are left to [teach] the world how the old people lived," Hicks laments, but, as Isbell suggests, his choice of vocation—his decision to become a professional storyteller and share his gift with audiences both inside and outside the environs of Beech Mountain—has assured that members of subsequent generations will still be able to access the old tales and continue the oral tradition (164). While it is true that a corpus of Jack Tales originally immigrated from Europe, in Appalachia they acquired a particular cultural resonance when narrated in Hicks's distinct style. Many storytellers who have heard Hicks perform have interiorized his stories and have incorporated them into their own repertoires. But this phenomenon is not limited to the Appalachian storytellers, for people far outside the region have also appropriated Hicks's versions of the Jack Tales and introduced them as symbols within their own communities. Thus his influence has spread far beyond his Beech Mountain homeland.

Two tellers of Jack Tales are especially representative: Frank Proffitt Jr. lives in Appalachia and is a member of Hicks's immediate family, while Jim May, though a native of Illinois, learned the Jack Tales from Hicks himself. Both men have created adaptations of Hicks's tales that retain traditional elements yet demonstrate the influence of their specific geographical region and culture.

The impact of Hicks's storytelling career includes the story of his acceptance beyond his home community. He began telling stories professionally in 1951 at Cove Creek School, located only a few miles from his home. As Isbell explains, a teacher named Jennie Love had been using Chase's *The Jack Tales* in her class and she wanted Hicks to demonstrate storytelling for the children. She paid him three dollars for every visit and he was so successful the other classes demanded a performance as well (28-29). Hicks reveals that "they said they was a-going to start a war here; said it wasn't fair to get Mister Hicks to tell stories just in [one] room" (30).

After his appearances at the Cove Creek School, the demand for Hicks's services grew until he began performing on a national level. In 1963, Folk Legacy Records produced a disc containing four of his Jack Tales. In 1973, the promoters of The National Storytelling Festival invited Hicks to perform during its inaugural event and have subsequently extended an invitation every year. In fact, Hicks is introduced at the festival as America's best known and most respected traditional storyteller. In 1983, Hicks received a National Heritage Fellowship from the National Endowment for the Arts Folklife Office—the highest award the United States has to offer to those citizens who are promoting and preserving such knowledge of the past. In *The Storyteller's Journey: An American Revival*, Sobol comments that Hicks is a traditional storyteller "who had that mysterious something extra: star quality" (111). Even now, in his later years when his performances are limited due to ill health, the festival audience fills Hicks's tent to capacity.

In an interview with Sobol, Duncan Williams, a Scottish storyteller, describes his first meeting with Hicks: "I've heard stories about Jack all my life; I've told hundreds o' stories about Jack; but today, I finally met Jack" (35). To many,

Hicks embodies the traits and personality of Appalachian Jack. Indeed, their histories seem to run parallel. Both Hicks's and Jack's families lived in poverty. Neither mother had much food for her family. Both boys faced life on their own terms. Hicks sacrificed his own interests in life—namely his education—to provide food and earn money for his family, just as Jack leaves home to find his fortune and returns with the bounty. In short, the two childhoods—one actual and one fictional—are spent in remarkably similar fashion.

Because of his influence over other storytellers, Hicks leaves obvious legacies to the tradition of the tales. His success as a teller of traditional tales is crucially important to his ability to present both himself and his home community on a national stage. In an interview with Sobol, Barbra Freeman comments on Hicks's first performance at the National Storytelling Festival:

> Ray was so nervous that he looked at the sky the whole time. And that microphone, and his voice, he was just shaking, you know; and his mouth was dry, and he was scared to pieces.
> And I thought to myself, and Connie [Regan-Blake] I know had the same thought, Boy, this seems cruel, you know, to bring somebody who is a front-porch storyteller out of their natural environment and subject them to a big microphone and big speakers and a great crowd of people. 'Cause this man is miserable. (101)

Fortunately, Hicks moved past his "growing pains" and developed the style of performance that has continued to draw vast numbers of people. Freeman continues:

> Of course, the next year…he was grabbing that microphone and in full control. In full tilt-boogie; so I kind of readjusted a little bit. I just said that was like growing pains; And people love it so much, and now Ray loves it so much. (101)

Hicks's success encourages a belief in the capacities of traditional "front-porch" storytelling. In fact, he remains a mentor or father figure to many within the storytelling community. Of his influence on storytelling, Hicks relates:

> Why it's becoming popular now. You'd hear about [the festival in Jonesborough] Tennessee? Well, now you see, I'se the one who got that started…the storytelling of the tales. Jack tales, was Ray's. I was the lead teacher. Now there's lots of storytellers, ye see. (McDermitt 9)

Sobol explains that tellers who meet him at festivals or visit his home on Beech Mountain "discover first hand how stories can function in a traditional community, household, and world view" (113-114). Because of his widespread influence, Hicks truly embodies the figure of the storyteller who, in Walter Benjamin's account, can encounter him/herself in another (109).

HICKS'S INFLUENCE ON BEECH MOUNTAIN STORYTELLERS

When Frank Proffitt Jr. began telling stories professionally, he followed a familiar family form. As a direct descendent of Council Harmon and the nephew of Ray Hicks, Proffitt Jr. could hardly avoid the family influence upon his storytelling technique. Unlike his immediate ancestors, however, Proffitt Jr. received a formal education, and Richard Chase's written versions of the Jack Tales also influenced the development of his oral style of narration. In fact, one of Chase's native informants was Frank Proffitt Sr. (Chase spells the name "Proffit.") Chase collected a version of AT 1525 "The Master Thief" from Proffitt Sr., entitled "Jack and the Old Rich Man," and printed it in the appendix of The Jack Tales.[11] As Carl Lindahl reports in "Jack, My Father, and Uncle Ray," Proffitt Jr. credits Chase with keeping his father's story alive (27). Although Proffitt Sr. may not have been as accomplished a teller as Hicks, his work is preserved and shared with the Beech Mountain community via the printed word.

Proffitt Jr.'s fundamental invention in reworking "Jack and the Old Rich Man" is his combination of the traditional oral style with the literary version. The model for this Jack Tale, AT 1525, presents a story in which a rich man puts a youth through a series of tests during which he must steal or be killed (Aarne and Thompson 431). Combining the forms of the tale has two effects: it gives Proffitt Jr. a form inclusive enough to embrace the variety of adaptations of AT 1525, and it allows him to express his own individuality while still working within the bounds of tradition.

At once traditional and personal, Proffitt Jr.'s version of "Jack and the Old Rich Man" brings together a mixture of conventions to demonstrate that this storyteller has mastered what both the oral and the written versions of the tale have to offer. The mixture appears most obviously to borrow from the adaptations of the tale presented by Hicks and Proffitt Sr. While in some respects the two adaptations are similar (both, for instance, show an awareness of the impoverished living conditions of the Beech Mountain area), they differ in the essentials. The first difference can be seen in the style of presentation. Hicks had learned and still performs his version of AT 1525, "The Doctor's Daughter" or "Jack and the Robbers," in a purely oral format while Proffitt Sr. has composed his adaptation in a written form. Secondly, Hicks includes several scenes and elements of action in his version that Proffitt Sr., presumably in order to keep the plot firmly centered upon the two title characters, eliminates. Finally, although many of the formulaic phrases that comprise the tales are shared by the two storytellers, several important formulas occur in one and not the other owing to differences in plot and character development.

While both men furnish crucial models for Proffitt Jr. in the development of his own version of AT 1525, he also creates something new. For example, Hicks and Proffitt Sr. present stories that deal with the poverty of the Appalachian community and issues of social justice—including the conflicts with authority inherent in the current social order and the necessity of individual rights. But Proffitt Jr.'s adaptation concerns many more levels of social justice, for it relates moral obligation both to individual human lives and to general society.

The storytelling style Proffitt Jr. adopts for "Jack and the Old Rich Man" typifies his ambition. Combining traditional storytelling elements from Hicks and Proffitt Sr., it overcomes both. In an interview with Lindahl, Proffitt Jr. says:

> [Proffitt Sr.] was not what you would call a storyteller, as compared to Ray [Hicks]. He could tell a good story and knew a lot of them—mostly stories to go with the songs and ballads. There were, for example, many Civil War Stories he learned from his father, handed down through the family from my great-grandfather, John Proffitt a "Southern Yankee" who served with the 13th Tennessee Cavalry, USA. He also heard many of them from his Uncle Noah. In other words, my father would hardly tell stories unless prompted in relation to a song or ballad. Ray tells them, or insists on telling them, on the spot, while my father was shy that way. He was more comfortable telling facts rather than fiction. He was a great "fact" or "true" storyteller—although he could be a fairly good liar when he wanted to [be]. (29)

Proffitt Jr. does not follow his father's speech pattern because he prefers his uncle's style. He admits that this may be due to Hick's "insistence" on telling a tale and his domination as "the storyteller" in the family. For whatever reason, Proffitt Sr. seems to have had little desire and less opportunity than Hicks to express himself through stories.

Proffitt Jr.'s clearest predecessor is Hicks. He readily admits:

> I tell "Jack and the Old Rich Man" in this style from my Uncle Ray Hicks...I try, or really do it without thinking. I use Ray's accent to a degree, because I have heard him so much and I am part Hicks, and it comes naturally I guess. (Lindahl 30)

Hicks's style, as Lindahl notes, "often runs sentences together in long, loping bounds of sound" (35). In his own style of storytelling Proffitt Jr.'s recognizes the patterns inherent in the traditional type of Beech Mountain storytelling Hicks represents. Because his life has been spent steeped in the atmosphere of Hicks's performances, he incorporates the voice of the elder generation effortlessly. Yet Proffitt Jr. also stretches the traditional form.

Though the deliberate assumption of Hicks's style serves at first to conceal the originality of his adaptation, Proffitt Jr. progresses beyond the traditional form by increasing the pace of his speech and providing only the briefest pauses between lines to unify the whole (Lindahl 35). But Proffitt Jr. avoids confusion by providing a cue at the end of a line that Lindahl describes as "an upward, almost questioning inflection on the last accent or last accented word" (35). Proffitt Jr.'s results, deliberate, ruminative, and profoundly original, combine the traditional elaborate form of oral composition with the simpler structure of a person reading a story aloud.

In all three adaptations of the tale the concern for social justice is evident, for a poor young man and his family must work for a rich man who treats them shabbily. Yet, toward the subject of injustice, Proffitt Sr. and Hicks have a slightly different attitude, one that is reflected in the opening passages of their tales. When Proffitt Jr. chooses to incorporate both Hicks's and Proffitt Sr.'s visions, he makes his meaning out of the tensions between them.

Proffitt Sr. opens his narrative with a passage that identifies the three main characters: "Jack and his mother worked for a old rich man for their Living. Jack found out where the old rich man kept his money and he concluded he would steal it" (Chase 195). Hicks's version differs slightly, but still manages to focus on the characters of Jack and the doctor who is Hicks's version of the Old Rich Man:

> Well, this one here I'm a-fixin to tell is about Jack and his parents. At this time they were a-rentin, a-stayin on this doctor's place, a-share croppin, and a-workin fer him a-doing everything that he said. Had to, you know. Gosh back at that time if you rented they, ye know people liked renters to work, and if you were a good and they'd git the advantage of ye and make you do all the work. They'll have ye work till ye can't stand up...(McDermitt 9)

In his opening, Proffitt Sr. does not dwell on the inequality between his characters; the abuse by the Old Rich Man is almost assumed—the only "proof" offered as to the quality of his character lies in his possession of a large amount of money. Proffitt Sr. seems to be relying upon a socially accepted prejudice in this regard—either the Old Rich Man must be in possession of money to which he is not entitled or the story would appear to be slanted to portray Jack as a villain. Indeed, Proffitt Sr. also describes Jack as "stealing" the money—a fact perhaps also seeming to cast his character in a negative light.

Although the Jack Tale is placed in a fictional setting, Hicks works from the beginning to create a narrative that is self-consciously reflective of an Appalachia where, as Lindahl notes, the depression continues to exist (32). Refraining from mentioning money in his opening passage, Hicks centers the narrative almost solely on the work ethic of the tenant farmers. In his story, more work is expected of Jack and his family than they are actually paid to produce. Hicks's comments reveal that this practice is considered socially acceptable and is even expected by the renters. Given their way, "they" (presumably the wealthy land owners) would work the tenant farmers until they dropped from physical exhaustion.

In his opening, Proffitt Jr. both invokes the earlier models and manages to augment them. He recounts:

> Well, this one's about where Jack and his mother worked for an Old Rich Man,and Jack, he found out where the Old Rich Man kept his money, and he concluded he's going to help hisself to some of it, since the old man hadn't been paying him and his mother nothing hardly, just bare enough to eat, and not, not nothing, no money on the side hardly, just a little, penny every now and then. (34)

In the opening line suggesting that this Appalachian Jack Tale will be something new, Proffitt Jr. blends the two versions to create a new synthesis at once centered on the aspect of theft and Jack's belief that something is owed to him and his family. Although Jack is a thief, because the Old Rich Man is withholding money, he is "helping" himself to what is owed by his employer. In specific and deliberate word choice, Proffitt Jr. develops in the tale the concept of social justice that a worker should be paid fairly for labor. In an interview with Lindahl, Proffitt Jr. explains that he wants the audience to realize "the Old Rich Man got what he deserved for being so stingy, treating Jack and his mother like that" (32).

The fundamental fact of Proffitt Jr.'s adaptation is a right of ownership referred to directly and kept constantly before the audience in direct dialogue between Jack and the Old Rich Man. The concept appears during their first exchange: when the Old Rich Man accuses Jack of stealing his money, Jack replies with great emphasis, "not your'n, but MINE" (37). A later exchange also addresses the issue of ownership:

> [Old Rich Man] said, "Being you think you're such a good robber and I'm gonna—there's one thing you've gotta do between now and tomorrow morning. You've got to steal off of me, or I'll have you hung or shot certain."
> And Jack said, "If I do, is it mine?"
> He said, "Yea-ah.
> It's yours if you can steal."
> Jack said, "What I got to steal?"
> He said, "You got to steal my saddle horse out of my stable tonight, with a saddle on it—my mare, out of the stable, between now and tomorrow morning, or I'll have you hung or shot, certain."
> Said, "If you do, it's yours." (37)

Proffitt Jr. offers a similar exchange between the two characters four more times in the narrative. Although the verbal strategy of repetition is by no means unique to Proffitt Jr's adaptation—it is a habit of oral literature that reaches into the very rhythm and logic of its development, by choosing to repeat the particular of the social injustice over and over, Proffitt Jr. raises the audience members' awareness of the exchange and draws their attention to the rights of ownership established between the two men.

While the opposition of a young man to an old one is a familiar Jack Tale technique, here Proffitt Jr.'s concern with social justice gives it a new resonance. Jack and the Old Rich Man embody opposite ends of life's spectrum. Their different ages result in radically different values made apparent when the challenges are issued. The Old Rich Man represents the nominal authority in the tale: he is rich, powerful, and can have Jack "shot" or "hung" as a thief. Jack is seemingly powerless in this situation—he makes certain to establish his legal "right" to steal and receives an oral agreement from the Old Rich Man. (In the tale, as is traditional, both men are assumed to have a certain degree of honor and will not renege on their given promise.) It is necessary, however, for Jack to obtain that verbal agreement; he requires the nominal authority of the Old Rich Man in order to "legally" steal.

At first the Old Rich Man uses his own possessions to create challenges for Jack. He remains within the bounds of the law and the limits of authority—anything offered to Jack as an object to steal originally belongs to the Old Rich Man. But when he demands that Jack steal Brother Dickie's money, the Old Rich Man

64   Ray Hicks and the Jack Tales

trespasses beyond the bounds of his authority. In the prologue to the Brother Dickie episode, the Old Rich Man issues the theft challenge:

> Old Rich Man flew mad and cussed him up one side and down the Other'n and said, "You-you think you're such a good robber?"
> Jack said, "I've done pretty good, ain't I?"
> Said, "Well, just one more thing...you gotta steal between now and tomorrow morning or I'll have you hung or shot certain."
> Jack said, "What's that?"
> And said, "You gotta steal all my Brother Dickie's money or I'll have you hung or shot certain."
> Jack said, "If I do, is it mine?"
> Said, "Yea-ah.
> It's your'n." (40-41)

This episode is largely Proffitt Jr.'s own innovation—Brother Dickie and his wife do not appear in Hick's version and are mentioned only briefly by Proffitt Sr. In Proffitt Jr.'s adaptation of the tale this is the largest episode—it is the theft challenge that entails the most time and detail in the narrative. The extra narrating time spent is significant because it allows Proffitt Jr. to express his own view that those in power often abuse it. Whatever authority the Old Rich Man possesses disappears completely when he orders Jack to steal from another party.

Because of the descriptive detail Proffitt Jr. invests in the narrative, Brother Dickie and his wife are not unknown victims—he is the local preacher and she is his wife of many years. Proffitt Jr. works to make them well-developed and completely believable characters. For example, after Jack appears as the Angel Gabriel and offers transport to heaven for a fee, Brother Dickie runs home to tell his wife about the marvelous opportunity. She is skeptical at first and their conversation dissolves into a pattern of argument that seems to form the basis of their relationship. Proffitt Jr. says:

> She's trying to tell him it was somebody trying to trick him, said, "That's somebody trying to fool you, trying to get all your money or something."
> Said, "You better watch it."
> He said, "No!" He said, "No!"
> Said, Brother Dickie said, "It's the Angel Gabriel.
> And," said—"All I need to go to paradise, to heaven—it's a one-way ticket to Gloryland—is just give him all my money and I'm on my way." Said, "You been telling me I'll split hell wide open. I'll show you."
> Said, "I may never get another chance like this."
> And she was argu-he was arguing, they was having it out, you know.

And, finally, she said, "Wait a minute!" He'd started to take all his money.
He said, "What?"
She said, "Just take half the money. He won't know the difference.
Just take half of it…"
Said, "Well, I reckon I'll go along with you on that." (42-43)

Although this exchange reveals the couple's interpersonal relationship, it also serves to reveal their characters. While Brother Dickie fears his reception in the afterlife, his wife likes to reinforce these fears by saying he will "split hell wide open" (43). Rather than focusing on the afterlife, she appears more concerned with their time in this world and does not want him to give up all of his money. But this is not a decision she can make—Brother Dickie is in charge of the family finances. Still, she is able to urge caution and suggests he compromise at first by presenting only half of the money. The decision ultimately lies with him, however, for she is in a subservient position because it is ultimately "his" money to spend or keep. Her voice of reason fades behind the force of Brother Dickie's foolish behavior.

By providing a slice-of-life that reveals the interpersonal dynamics between Brother Dickie and his wife, Proffitt Jr. establishes sympathy for their loss. Jack's crime is not perpetrated against a faceless statistic—Jack knows the people and can recognize them as members of his community.

Jack is then trapped between the conflicting demands of society at large and those of the Old Rich Man, between two imperative and mutually exclusive authorities. He cannot follow the Rich Old Man's orders and save his own life without breaking the law and stealing from Brother Dickie (a crime that Proffitt Jr. indicates in his narrative as being punishable by death). Jack is trapped not by random events but by a situation in which all roads could lead to death.

Although Jack seems in an impossible situation, he receives reassurance from the Old Rich Man that if he succeeds in the task he has set, the money will legally belong to him. To Jack, the Old Rich Man's claim is plausible because he is an insider from a social sphere about which Jack inevitably feels uncertain. Although the audience may be aware of more complicated legal ramifications, Jack does not yet realize that the Old Rich Man has overreached his authority. "While I don't condone thievery," Proffitt Jr. explains elsewhere, "Jack had to do it, because it was forced on him. He did it to survive" (Lindahl 32). This comment mirrors Hicks's opinion of Jack in the story—that he had to steal to survive (McDermitt 8). The problem thus does not lie with the boy, but with the Old Rich Man who establishes the rules of the game.

The theft-challenge of Brother Dickie's money is the moment of crisis between Jack and the Old Rich Man. Although several other theft-challenges follow, this one is the point in the narrative where the reversal of fortunes begins and builds until the Old Rich Man is forced to work for Jack (Proffitt Jr. 55).

In establishing the reversal of fortune, Proffitt Jr. is more subtle than his predecessors. Proffitt Sr. is the least subtle of the three, for his characters continue in the same way until, abruptly at the end, Jack is revealed as having gained more wealth than the Old Rich Man. Hicks dramatizes the reversal more fully. He hinges the fall of the Old Rich Man (Doctor) on a violent moment in the action; there, when the older man shoots at Jack and displays a blatant disregard for the law, he gives Jack a way to beat him. Hicks recounts the violence in a dialogue between the old man and his wife:

> An his wife said, "You killed Jack."
> He [the Doctor] said, "I think so. I heared his body hit the ground."
> Said, "You better go check,"
> He went out and checked. Seed that blood an come back an said, "Yeah, I killed the rascal."
> He said, "He's out there. God," he said, "looks like he's had plenty of blood."
> Said, "God, it's all over his body."
> "Well," she said, "you better go git your neighbors and see if you can hide his [?] body. Doc, the law will have you in no time." (McDermitt 15)

Having overreached his authority in a spectacular fashion by supposedly killing Jack and attempting to hide his actions from the law, the Old Rich Man provides Jack the means to achieve his desire and marry the Doctor's daughter. The Old Rich Man has actually missed Jack with his three shots, but three bullet holes in Jack's cap are the physical proof of attempted murder needed to secure the Old Rich Man/Doctor's downfall.

The reversal of fortune in Proffitt Jr.'s tale lies in the Brother Dickie episode. Everything that follows, including a segment that mirrors Hicks's violent confrontation between the title characters, only adds to the Old Rich Man's downfall. Prior to the Brother Dickie episode, the Old Rich Man had not worried about his own welfare; afterwards his concern lies in being cleaned "out of everything now" (Proffitt Jr. 53). Eventually, as in Proffitt Sr.'s adaptation, Proffitt Jr. has the Old Rich Man fall so far socially and economically that he needs to work for Jack's family (55).

The oral formulaic expressions used by the three tellers also serve to highlight the conflict of authority and the assertion of individual rights in the Jack Tale. It is not uncommon for formulaic expressions to be used throughout an oral art form or literary work directly influenced by oral tradition because it provides a rhythmic emphasis and draws the audience members' attention to specific information or actions by the characters. In their versions of AT 1525, the three Appalachian tellers repeat formulaic expressions throughout their tales to draw attention to the conflict between Jack and the Old Rich Man.

One verbal formula repeated in all three versions of AT 1525 is Jack's question, "If I do, is it mine?" Jack asks it after every theft-challenge issued by the Old Rich Man. Beyond its plot function, Jack's requiring assurance that the theft he is about to perpetrate will result in a "legal" transference of goods reveals something about his social standing. The Old Rich Man has obvious authority over Jack and the young man is aware of this fact. His inquiry reinforces the social relations mainly because the pattern is so evident.

Another verbal formula recurring in all three versions of the tale pertains to Jack's desire to establish rights of possession. Each time the Old Rich Man tries to reclaim any property, Jack blocks him with a reassertion of his rights. All three storytellers use a variation of the statement, "It's not yours, but it's mine." The formula functions to satisfy the legal issues surrounding possession of the stolen items and to justify Jack's theft of them to both the Old Rich Man and the audience.

A third verbal formula found in all three versions highlights the upward shift in social position that Jack's family experiences after they obtain material wealth. After the first theft, the Old Rich Man comes to Jack's home and wants to know why the family is not working for him. Jack's parents tell him that "we are just as independent as you. We do not need to work for you anymore." It is important to note that all three tellers use the word "independent" to describe Jack's family. They are not yet as wealthy as the Old Rich Man, so their economic status is not equal to his. But they do not have to work for him, so they are no longer dependent upon him.

In their versions of AT 1525, the three Appalachian tellers also use plot formulas to draw attention to the conflict between Jack and the Old Rich Man. Because Proffitt Sr. centers his plot around the contest between Jack and the Old Rich Man, he shows just how serious is Jack's situation, one fraught with life and death consequences. If Jack fails, he will lose his life.

The threat against Jack's life does not appear in Hicks's version of the tale. His plot hinges on Jack's ignorance of social hierarchy and his bid to secure the Old Rich Man/Doctor's daughter in marriage. Hicks's version dramatizes tensions created by the competing demands of social standing, duty to family, and self-

68   Ray Hicks and the Jack Tales

advancement. The Old Rich Man/Doctor places a price on his daughter's hand in marriage—her suitors must have a thousand guineas in order to court her (McDermitt 9). The continued prosperity and social standing of the Old Rich Man/Doctor's biological line depends upon his ability to make an advantageous marriage match for his daughter.

Hicks does not place Jack in a life-and-death struggle with the Old Rich Man/Doctor until the final conflict forces him to place his life on the line. Jack merely undergoes a series of tests to prove his worth as a prospective bridegroom and is thrust into life and death situations by outsiders. For example, when Jack is on the road seeking to earn the thousand guineas, he is captured by a band of thieves who force him to steal by literally placing a gun to his head. "Jack wasn't a man like the robbers was, holding a gun," Hicks comments, "he just got caught in it" (McDermitt 8). Yet Hicks also fosters suspicion of ambiguity in Jack's moral character—rather than merely saving his life, he retains money from his services as a thief. Although Jack is not an armed robber and tricks his victims out of their goods, he still gains monetarily from their misfortune. Although Jack started stealing in order to survive, he later uses the tainted money to try and claim his bride.

In his adaptation of AT 1525, Proffitt Jr. tries to join the two distinct elements of his predecessors. In plot, his tale uses Proffitt Sr.'s battle between Jack and the Old Rich Man, and, in theme, he highlights the moral ambiguity evident in Hicks's creation. The combination divides Proffitt Jr.'s story into two contrasting segments. In the first, Jack has his competition with the Old Rich Man. In the second, Jack steals from Brother Dickie.

Proffitt Jr. echoes all three formulas in his tale. The formulas provide the closest tie to Proffitt Sr.'s adaptation of the tale, emphasizing that the two main characters are Jack and the Old Rich Man. Although Brother Dickie and his wife are fascinating characters, Jack's main battle is with the Old Rich Man. If Jack fails, he will lose his life.

The Brother Dickie episode raises the same questions as Hicks about the ambiguity in Jack's moral character. Is Jack morally responsible for his theft of Brother Dickie's money? He is incapable of extricating himself through any other means—if he does not steal, he will be killed and if he does steal, he runs the risk of being caught and killed. Jack's act also raises the problem of judgment. He makes a terrible mistake in trusting the Old Rich Man's authority, but to a young farm boy, the Old Rich Man's authority must seem absolute. Proffitt Jr. supplies evidence both for Jack's guilt and his incapacity to behave like a hero; he leaves the audience members with an uneasy uncertainty about the extent of his culpability.

The brilliance of Proffitt Jr.'s adaptation of "Jack and the Old Rich Man" comes from a density of context as passages and episodes play against others and deepen in relation to the larger oral and literary traditions that he evokes. He allows the audience members not only to confront their own confusion of social justice and individual rights, but also to confront the contradictions in their own ideas about moral obligation. The story prompts listeners to question their own roles in society: how they are to envision them, to withstand economic and social pressures, and to make their lives fruitful.

HICKS'S INFLUENCE BEYOND BEECH MOUNTAIN

"Thank you, Ray Hicks, for telling me about Jack," Jim May comments in *The Farm on Nippersink Creek*. Many storytellers from outside Appalachia like May have been introduced to the Jack Tales by Hicks. These tellers have attempted to follow the tradition and share the knowledge of the Beech Mountain residents. What is problematic, however, is the degree of accuracy the non-native tellers can, or even should, maintain. "You don't tell the tales just from the way they [are] put down; ye tell em to suit your own, your own feelings, the way I tell em," Hicks explains (McDermitt 6). This is a cultural chasm across which the Appalachian and non-Appalachian storytellers attempt to connect. The Jack Tales told by people outside of the Beech Mountain community evolve from the Appalachian tradition to encompass the cultural traditions from other areas of the United States.

For his Jack Tale, "Soldier Jack Meets the Purple Bogies," May adapts Hicks's tale "Whickety-Whack, into My Sack," but he changes radically what he uses and instills a cultural framework from the midwest onto the Appalachian base. Both works portray Jack as a man on a quest, but while Hicks's story balances fortune against misfortune, suggesting that both are a part of life, May's story becomes a study in the mistreatment of Jack by untouchable and superior social forces. Hicks also places Jack within a home community, providing him support and companionship, while May leaves Jack on the outskirts of society desperately searching for a home.

Hicks begins his narrative by having Jack start his journey home. He states:

70   Ray Hicks and the Jack Tales

> Well, Jack went into the army and stayed thirty years. And at that time, all
> you got when they discharged you was two loaves of bread. And when they
> discharged Jack, they give 'im two loaves of bread and he headed off into the
> woods, tryin' to git home. (Hicks 10)

This is not an unusual payment—Hicks creates a non-personal statement ("all
you got") to demonstrate that Jack is not receiving any special mistreatment. Jack
merely takes his two loaves and heads home.

> It is just this equitable balance that May's opening avoids:
> In those days Jack had just gotten out of the army. Now, when you got out of
> the King's army, they didn't give you any money. They just gave Jack two
> loaves of bread and it was white bread and it wasn't even sliced! Jack had been
> in the army for thirty years and that was his commission—two loaves of bread.
> ("Soldier Jack Meets the Purple Bogies")

May's additions to the traditional narrative are evident from the first. He explains
that the King (an authority figure no longer recognized in the United States) pays
his soldiers in loaves of bread instead of money. Because it is "white" and not
sliced, the quality of the bread seems suspect. May then reiterates that Jack had
given thirty years of his life for those two loaves of bread—implying that the
trade seems unfairly weighted toward the benefit of the King. Jack thus suffers
great misfortune from the very beginning.

What is even more interesting is May's omission of Jack's "home." After leav-
ing the army, Jack does not have a home community with which to reintegrate.
This seemingly small omission reveals a vast difference between Hicks, a native
Appalachian teller, and May, a non-native teller, as they attempt to tell the same
story. The Jack Tales from Beech Mountain are all set in an isolated sphere—no
matter how far Jack travels, the geography and the customs he encounters mirror
life in Appalachia. In *Orality and Literacy*, Walter Ong suggests that the orally-
based transmission of knowledge contributes to a type of isolationist behavior
within a community. Unlike written literature, oral art forms do not allow the
storage of knowledge as an entity separate from the larger community (42). "Oral
cultures," Ong believes, "must conceptualize and verbalize all their knowledge
with more or less close reference to the human life-world" (42). Jack is never far
from home because it always travels with him.

By telling an Appalachian tale, May has passed beyond the prescribed boundaries of his own area (the Midwest) and has entered a new and unfamiliar territory. Jack is not returning "home" because the storyteller who is controlling the

narrative has never lived there. The frame of reference differs enough that Jack is left wandering about looking for a familiar area to settle, yet is frustrated in his efforts because the two communities do not combine.

Reinforcing the perception that Jack is caught between two cultures is May's statement of the traveler's condition after he has spent the day on the road. May explains that "Jack, well, he walked all day. He got hungry. He got tired. He wasn't sure where he was going to stay that night or what he was going to eat" ("Soldier Jack Meets the Purple Bogies"). Exhausted and with no sustenance available to him, Jack searches for food and shelter and eventually spies a rooming house in the distance. May states:

Well, Jack went up to that house and knocked on the door.

> A lady came to the door and she said, "Yes?" He said, "Hi, I'm Jack. I just got out of the army. They didn't give me any money when I got out of the army, but they gave me two loaves of bread. Of course I gave those away to an old beggar up the road. Fact there was two beggar men and I gave both my loaves of bread away. But I thought I could stay here tonight, maybe get something to eat and rested up and tomorrow I'd go get a job. And I'll pay you back."
> She said, "Jack, if you got no money, you got no place to stay neither," and she slammed the door. Well, Jack, he didn't know what to do now. ("Soldier Jack Meets the Purple Bogies")

Jack's good deeds in life gain him nothing in the eyes of the landlady (a native of the region in which Jack is seeking to live). He is rejected out of hand because he is deemed unsuitable. Jack has not found a place to stay or a home community to enter because of his lack of material success. Money is worth more in the eyes of the community than the intangible qualities of character—such as being a loyal soldier or having a generous nature. Only when Jack can pay his way will he have a place to stay and the comforts of a home—listed by May as a bath, a clean bed to sleep in, a turkey dinner, and biscuits and gravy for breakfast ("Soldier Jack Meets the Purple Bogies").

This lack of hospitality is markedly different from May's own Spring Grove, Illinois, upbringing. In *The Farm on Nippersink Creek*, May relates the story of the Good Samaritan and describes how his family put the parable into action by taking in a homeless man one Christmas Eve. May explains:

> [My mother's] great-uncle Matt...had been in the California Gold Rush of 1849. He hadn't found any gold but he found out what it meant to almost starve to death and to rely on handouts to survive. He had told my grand-

72   Ray Hicks and the Jack Tales

> mother never to let anyone go hungry, and my grandmother had told my
> mother. (47)

This is the sense of community May's Jack seems to be searching for throughout the narrative—one that he never achieves. It is interesting to note that this rejection does not occur in Hick's narrative. It is unique to May's adaptation. Hicks has Jack approach the rooming house only after he has caught several turkeys that he can barter for his lodgings. Hicks's Jack seems to understand the fact that there is no "free ride" in the community and that he has to pay as he goes along. May's Jack only seems to recognize this fact when the door is slammed in his face.

After Jack's overnight stay at the rooming house, Hicks has him continue upon his journey: "Well, the next mornin', he started out and purty soon made it home. He went to a-workin; on his cabin, repairing his old home place to live in 'til he got to where he could do better" (11). Hicks has Jack work at his own house until he finds an opportunity to better himself. If he is able to run off the ghosts—the undesirable tenants of a big farm—he will receive clear title to the house and land.

May describes the same situation:

> Jack has such a good experience at there at the rooming house he thought he'd stay in that town. Look for a place to live permanent. Now he heard there was a man outside of town. He had a house and he was going to give that house away. ("Soldier Jack Meets the Purple Bogies")

Jack's "good experience" with the town occurs after he earns enough money to pay his own way. Money, it seems, is the key to social acceptance, but only for a short time. Even though Jack wants to stay in the town—in the community—the only house available to him is located "outside of town." Even if he can somehow manage to acquire the house, he will still be an outsider in the community.

The deliberate placement of Jack outside the social structure of the town makes May's tale a unique creation. This setting functions as more than physical topography. May creates a complex symbol that reveals the thin line that Jack must walk as he tries to bridge the two cultures. At first this remote house could seem ideal to an Illinois storyteller who has described his longing for just such an isolated place in *The Farm on Nippersink Creek*. Instead of having his life "regimented and closely guarded by community elders" May's Jack is able to escape from the town to live "where the laws of nature ruled" (May 155). Jack could remain "set apart, away from the responsibilities of job and family, to immerse [himself] in the immediacy of great natural forces, to hold silent vigil" (May

156). Although at first this seems an ideal placement to one who longs to escape life's responsibilities, in the end the lack of community ties becomes a sentence of "banishment"(May 155). Indeed, it seems that Jack's culturally-defined role has shifted once again, but this time, unlike AT 328, there is no need for a maligned giant in the narrative; Jack has taken over the role of the ultimate outsider.

Although May closely follows the traditional Appalachian style, he also utilizes contemporary images to create his adaptation of the tale. For example, Hicks describes Jack's adversaries in the haunted house as "six little black devils [who] each had a sword apiece, and a deck of playing cards apiece" (11).

May's description of the adversaries differs significantly:

> Purple smoke began to billow out of that fireplace and then a purple ball of flame. And out of that purple ball of flame stepped a purple bogie…and then there were five…of the meanest, purplest bogies you ever saw. ("Soldier Jack Meets the Purple Bogies")

The characters May creates are reminiscent of images from modern cartoons. The images are more contemporary than Hicks's black devils (and more politically correct). Yet the purple bogies are not simply colorful ornamentations; like Hicks's black devils, they are pivotal characters in the narrative and serve as the primary villains. But Hicks's black devils and May's purple bogies differ on more than a descriptive level. Their encounter also serves to highlight the different forces operating on the two heroes.

The episode with the black devils once again demonstrates how Hicks's story balances fortune against misfortune. After emerging from the fireplace, the black devils beg Jack to play cards with them. He then wins all of their money, so they try to kill him. Jack fights off the black devils' attack and then captures them in his sack (11). Jack's winning streak is tempered by the attempt on his life and his streak of fortune/misfortune remains in balance.

May's episode highlights the mistreatment of Jack by the purple bogies. They force him to play cards and, even if he wins, threaten to eat him. Jack has no chance to determine his own destiny. Once again he is at the mercy of superior forces who are striving against him. His only outlet is to comment to the purple bogies with great irony that the situation "seems fair" ("Soldier Jack Meets the Purple Bogies").

On a certain level May's adaptation of "Soldier Jack Meets the Purple Bogies" make sense only as part of the linguistic and social code of a particular time and place. As May explains in *The Farm on Nippersink Creek*, the longing to be self-

74   Ray Hicks and the Jack Tales

sufficient, to be beyond the laws of mankind, to escape the boundaries of society and to set himself into the "immediacy of great natural forces" has shaped his life in Spring Grove, Illinois (154-156). Because Jack has taken over the role as the ultimate outsider, like the giant in AT 328, he is treated in a less than equitable manner. Not only do the bogies believe that they have the "moral" right to steal Jack's property and then to kill him because of his outsider status, but, as Jane Yolen reveals in *Touch Magic*, it is virtually incumbent upon them to do so (106). Yet Jack is still the hero and, following the traditional style of the narrative, must prevail over the seemingly superior forces of the purple bogies.

In "Soldier Jack Meets the Purple Bogies," May translates the complexities of a cultural situation into physical ones, but it is essential to the narrative that the audience never simply discards the literal level in apprehending the meaning it contains. Rather, the cultural differences May brings to the tale shine through the traditional narrative he adapts from Hicks, giving it a particular radiance of meaning. "I think of telling stories as an attempt to establish a community," May explains in *The Farm on Nippersink Creek*, and he attempts to bridge the Appalachian and Midwestern traditions and create a community that includes aspects of both cultures (14). Yet in the story, the road Jack travels ultimately spans the two cultures and the audience members learn much about the difficulties in finding a comfortable home in either world.

Storytellers tend to take from their predecessors what they can best use for themselves, and Hicks's tales offer various possibilities to different individuals. Hicks's versions of the Jack Tales have become a model for tellers to absorb and reshape, as he has absorbed and reshaped the tales of his ancestors. This refashioning of Hicks's Jack Tales will develop at a faster pace as subsequent generations lose contact with the environment and with the conditions upon which his tales depend for meaning, making it easier to mistake the part for the whole and drop part of the meaning. Retaining many kinds of knowledge—historical, philosophical, religious, and regional—is necessary to see what Hicks intends to impart in the tales. Central to this awareness is an understanding of the Beech Mountain community and the life of one of its residents—Ray Hicks.

Conclusion

"He is our Singer of Tales."

—Albert B. Lord

In *Story, Performance, and Event*, Richard Bauman asserts that "the student of oral literature, no less than the scholar of written literature, confronts individual folk [artists] and unique works of literary creation, worthy of critical attention as such, as artists and works of art" (8-9). The premise of this study supports Bauman's assertion and posits that Ray Hicks is just such an artist and his Appalachian Jack Tales are just such creations.

The adventures of an everyman hero named Jack derive from a Western European narrative cycle and are the oldest folktales to survive in the North American oral tradition. In the twenty-first century, the Jack Tales continue to retain their place at the forefront of Western oral tradition. The stories have an undeniable longevity—the first recorded print-version in English of a Jack Tale had been published during the fifteenth century—and still are significant cultural elements in the modern world for many different nations. In part this is due to the degree of adaptability of the stories. Over the centuries the tales of Jack and his adventures have tended to absorb the interests, values, and mores of the culture in which they are operating. For example, Jack and the Beanstalk can be found in over thirty countries, yet each adaptation contains specific details that elaborate different cultural perspectives. Jack's dilemmas are reshaped and his character changes, but each variation endures with something of the original tale intact. Because of their capacity for variation, the Jack Tales truly offer almost unlimited possibilities to the storytellers.

The origin of most of the Jack Tales from the Appalachian area can be traced back to the English tales that traveled across the ocean with the original settlers of the new country. Travelers from England during the late eighteenth and early nineteenth century, like Rev. Dr. Joseph Doddridge and Samual Kercheval, provide evidence that the American tales mirror to a great degree the Jack Tales found in the English chapbooks of the day. Traditional elements of English stories, such as Kings to head the government, and traditional English words, such

76   Ray Hicks and the Jack Tales

as guineas, that appear in the Appalachian tales also demonstrate a link between the two cultures.

Although the Jack Tales are part of an international tradition, Hicks adaptations are filled with Appalachian culture, topography, and values. In Hicks' view, storytelling is not an activity that can be separated from daily existence. The Jack Tales are part of Hicks' cultural heritage and he expresses a feeling of guardianship toward the tales—a belief that he is promoting the continuing relevance of the stories.

In *The Last Chivaree*, Robert Isbell explains how Hicks' attitude toward the Jack Tales had seeped into his consciousness as a young boy:

> As [Hicks] hoed potatoes and gathered wood, he thought of the stories told to him by the fires of a mountain winter. He was not aware that these same tales might have been recited to children by peat fires in another country in another time. He was driven by the sense, however, that he was divinely appointed to preserve the stories, to perpetuate the ways of his beloved people. He keenly felt the challenge of passing along the old ways to new generations. As he worked in the fields he told over to himself ballads and tales that might date back hundreds of years—kept alive by pioneers who came to a new country and continued the old traditions even as they created new adventures, new songs, new stories (78-79).

Hicks views himself as being in a line of descent from storytellers of previous generations and he claims a kinship by preserving and perpetuating the stories. There is a strong sense of community in his work—passing along the old ways to a new generation. The renditions of his inherited repertory of Jack Tales represents an emergent interaction between community life and narrative life, between worldview and narrative view, between the drama of daily life and the narrative drama of storytelling. In listening to Hicks one can realize not only the self-consciousness of the interconnection between life in the Appalachian Mountains and the narrative life of the Jack Tales, but also how strong a sense of community is formed with the members of an Appalachian audience.

Hicks' uniquely Appalachian tales, when performed before members of the local community, present the audience members with the knowledge that there is a common cultural ground on which to meet. Hicks performs his tales with a due concern for his audience members' interests and needs, filled with the confidence that he will be listened to and his topics lie within the hearers' experience and comprehension.

The way that Hicks has enhanced the Jack Tales through his manner of story-telling—the nature of his performance, his voice and mimicry, the stimulus of the audience and his response—have been explored in the previous pages. Of equal importance to this study is the setting of these tales—the background of the Appalachians that makes Hicks' Jack Tales a unique creation.

In every story Hicks presents his audience with one of the great places of fiction—like Twain's Mississippi or Dickens' London. The area comes to life as Hicks describes its farmhouses, shacks, barn yards, woods, rivers, fields, and towns. The Appalachian mountain area dominates the tales, yet is not simply an image; it is also a functional setting for Hicks' purposes. By confining all of his action to one terrain—the Appalachian version of Jack never leaves his home territory no matter how far he travels—Hicks achieves a unity of place which markedly adds in the creation of dramatic effects.

One example of a typical Hicks' setting is found in his version of "The Doctor's Daughter" or "Jack and the Robbers." The story begins with Jack as a sharecropper on the Doctor's farm. He falls in love with the Doctor's daughter and must leave to seek his fortune if he wishes to marry her (McDermitt 9). Hicks continues:

> An so he took off, left home. Didn't tell where'n the hair nor the tail he was a-goin. And he went off. Got in the woods at that time not many people near and got lost. He got lost and didn't known a hair'n the tail where he was at. An so along about ten or eleven o'clock in the night he was goin down a holler a-feelin in the dark of the woods a-wonderin what he would do to live. That it was dark as dungeon. That he was hungry and so weak an hit a-rain—an hit a-lookin like thunderin, an it was going to go rainin on him at any time. An with the wild animals in the woods to eat 'im up (McDermitt 10).

After beginning his quest, Jack finds himself lost in the woods that cover the mountains. He has lost his bearings and, in the darkness, the woods begin to develop a sinister potential. Jack is also hungry, he is weak, and the rain is not far off. Several man-eating animals share the woods with him.

Hicks proceeds with the narrative:

> An directly happen to see a little light a-shinin way down in the woods. That holped him, and he 'ginnin to tire, and got down through there an come to this light in the woods gettin closer. An when he got to it, it was a little house way back in them woods.

An he pecked—he went up to the door and the rain was a-runnin down. It
started rainin, a-pourin down off the eave of the house in his shirt, just a-
drownin him yet. An his hair all stuck to his head.
An so this little woman come out. An she said, "What are you here fer?"
He said, "I'm lost. I'm lost, lady. I'm lost. If you'd be my friend, I'm lost. An
could you do something to help me?"
She said, "Oh, gosh." Said, "This is a highway robber's house." Said, "They
caught me to stay with them, an I have to stay with them looks like." Says,
"There's no way out to keep their house here. Keep everything a-goin while
they've gone." Said, "They kill everybody that comes here." Said, "They say
dead people tell no tales."
An so he said, "Well, bedad, I'd just as soon be killed as to drown out here in
this rain," an just walked on in by her. "By golly, I'm froze. I'm hungry and
I'm wet and I'm froze an I feel like I've half drownded" (McDermitt 10).

Hicks translates Jack's physical journey through the woods into a complex moral
situation. The darkness of the setting suggests a moral blindness inherent in the
area and Jack's "lost" statement reveals his loss of purpose. When Jack is asked,
"What are you here for?" he does not provide any information about his
quest—he is just "lost" (McDermitt 10). The purpose of his quest—to earn
enough money to marry his true love—dissolves when he looses his physical orientation in the world. The light in the woods leads not toward Jack's salvation
and the fulfillment of his promise to the Doctor's daughter, but towards his even-
tual career as a robber.

The function of the Appalachian setting goes beyond its physical topography
in the way it is characterized by Hicks. It is clearly a complex symbol that affects
every person who resides there. Hicks talks about the here and the now, about the
Appalachians and Appalachian life, and he counts on his audience members to
focus on Appalachia—with its particular problems to confront and a communal
destiny to pursue.

Within Hicks' lifetime the Appalachian area has undergone rapid and radical
transformation. The community of his youth no longer exists. Even the immediate environs of Beech Mountain have altered with the passage of time. Isbell
describes a drive he shared with Hicks and Rosa Hicks:

We drive past a large, listing barn that was once a cheese factory; it was one of
the few enterprises in the area when Ray was a boy. After this there is a fork in
the road and a brick church close by.
"This used to be a wood church, were we went," says Rosa…
"Now there," Ray points. "See that big barn? It sits right where I went to
school" (Isbell 170-171).

Cultural transformations tend to keep pace with such physical transformations and in Appalachia have resulted in the reduction of opportunities for continuing the oral tradition. For example, Hicks main outlet for his stories in the past had been private performances in his neighbors' homes. With the advent of a technological innovation such as television, these "home" performances no longer provided the draw of exclusive entertainment and began to fade away. Hicks explains:

> They welcomed me to come to their homes, and then the otherns would come, and gosh I'd have crowds of children. The room would be full.
> That was before television come in the mountains. Now adder [after] television come and cut it down a lot. Television ruined it.
> They got me to come to some of their homes.
> An I got there, and they got television an they got it turned on so loud, they quit listening to me and I couldn't tell no tale, an I quit. An they just thought they wanted me to tell tales. You can't tell a tale with a television a goin. And you can't do nothin like that when your audience is looking at something else (McDermitt 5).

To tell his tales effectively, Hicks requires his listeners' full attention. Television as a medium for entertainment changed the social code and drew people away from the traditional entertainment of the oral art forms.

Such advances in social and technological elements have always been a part of human existence. In the face of such an inevitable force, it is necessary for a storyteller like Hicks to change his techniques and ways of expression in order to maintain the tradition and pass the tales along to the next generation of storytellers. The stories will not survive without listeners, and when the audience changes, a teller must adapt without losing the rich heritage invested in the tradition. In some instances, seeking out audiences from beyond the home territory helps to preserve "Appalachian" knowledge, customs, and beliefs.

Hicks has survived as a storyteller by actively seeking out new audiences. His appearances at schools, at festivals, and his willingness to talk to collectors of folklore have helped to ensure the preservation and the perpetuation of the Appalachian Jack Tale tradition. He has succeeded in adapting his stories so that they will be as captivating to audiences unfamiliar with the Appalachian community in which they originally thrived. For example, while Hicks includes traditional elements and descriptions, he will also present an explanation of regional terms to the audience. In "The Doctor's Daughter" or "Jack and the Robbers," Hicks utilizes this technique to explain the difference between "guineas" and the modern term "dollars:"

> You could call it, but it was a thousand guineas back then the guineas it could mean, if it was a thousand, it would mean ten dollars. Like they counted by the pennies. A hundred pennies was a dollar they called a penny a guinea, is the best I can remember...a hundred guineas, that would be a dollar (McDermitt 9).

Hicks changes his Jack Tale for audience members that are not familiar with native Appalachian terms and concepts. He uses the adaptations and additions to keep the legacy of the Jack Tales alive.

By performing his variations of the Jack Tales both inside and outside of his home community, Hicks has been able to influence the next generation of storytellers. "I was the lead teacher," Hicks admits, "now there's lot's of storytellers, ye see" (McDermitt 9). Many storytellers have interiorized Hick's tales and have incorporated the stories into their own repertoires. For instance, Frank Proffitt, Jr., a native Appalachian, tells Jack Tales that contain distinct elements of Hicks' style. In "Jack and the Old Rich Man," Hicks' influence on Proffitt, Jr.'s style of narration can be observed through several aspects, including vocal patterns and oral formulas. Jim May, a native of Illinois, attempts to connect with Hicks' versions of The Jack Tales across a cultural barrier. As he demonstrates in "Soldier Jack Meets the Purple Bogies," May adds elements to Hicks' narrative and installs a cultural framework from the Midwest onto the Appalachian base. The cultural differences enhance May's tale and help to provide meaning.

Because Hicks has been willing to share his Jack Tales with such a wide variety of audiences, his influence had spread beyond his Beech Mountain homeland. "I liked to tell [stories] to people that wanted em told, that enjoyed hearin them," Hicks admits (McDermitt 9). His enthusiasm and skill as a storyteller has allowed Hicks to bring an ancient body of oral literature to all types of audiences—from those who live in Appalachia and are highly familiar with the interests and concerns of the culture to those outside audiences who are unfamiliar with the stories, the language, and the culture in which the tales had developed.

Bauman believes that there exists individual artists within the oral tradition and unique works of oral art that are worthy of critical attention (8-9). Hicks is just such an oral artist working in the still-living Appalachian oral tradition of Jack Tales. While it is true that the Jack Tales have existed for many years and variations of the tales can be found in oral and literary works of many cultures, each culture—indeed each storyteller—adds new dimensions and nuances to the tales while still preserving the overall tradition. In Western society, literacy provides a way of preserving the essential lore of a culture, but the strength of storytelling in its current form lies in the participants' recognition that oral artists can move beyond the confines of the print medium and focus their works in oral composition. Both the artist and the audience can affect the composition of a story during a performance, creating a shared event that is unique. And, although some adaptation and interpretation can occur, the storytellers continue to work within the bounds of tradition.

As a storyteller from Appalachia, Hicks is part of the Jack Tales tradition. Yet one of the unique qualities of his work is that his stories emerge saturated with the events of his own life. Hicks' tales express his consciousness, modulating from story to story as he moves through life, yet always maintaining the qualities that answer to his own particular worldview. In the preceding pages I have attempted to demonstrate that Hicks merges his own persona into that of Jack's, seeming to share the trickster's thoughts, actions, and emotions.

"I'm Jack," Hicks asserts (McDermitt 8). The identification is not so much drawn from his material as imposed on it. The voice from the stage creates the reality for the audience members and the will of the narrator shapes his creation. And—with the numerous awards, books, audio-tapes, television and newspaper interviews, and researchers braving the back roads of Beech Mountain in order to listen and record his words—it appears that a great many people also agree with Hicks' claim and view him as the closest thing to the living embodiment of "Jack" that contemporary society has to offer.

"The Singer of Tales" is the term coined by Lord for artists within the living tradition of South Slavic oral poetry as well as other living traditions. Hicks has worked to preserve the living Appalachian tradition. He has infused the Jack Tales with elements of his life, his culture, his values, and his beliefs. He has worked to ensure that future generations will continue telling the tales. Hicks is a "singer" who, even after his death in 2003, will be remembered through his "song;" as long as the Jack Tales tradition endures the tales will be infused with the essential lore of his existence in Appalachia.

Works Cited

Aarne, Antti., and Stith Thompson. *The Types of the Folktale: A Classification and Bibliography.* Helsinki: Academia Scientiarum Fennica, 1987.

Altick, Richard D. *Victorian People and Ideas.* New York: W.W.Norton, 1973.

Anthony, Piers. *Isle of Women.* New York: Tom Doherty Associates, Inc., 1993.

Barthes, Roland. *Image, Music, Text.* Trans. Stephen Heath. New York: Hill and Wang, 1997.

Bauman, Richard. *Story, Performance, and Event: Contextual Studies of Oral Narrative.* Cambridge: Cambridge UP, 1986.

Benjamin, Walter. "The Storyteller: Reflections on the Works of Nikolai Leskov." *Illuminations.* New York: Schocken, 1968. 83-109.

Brians, Paul. *Bawdy Tales From the Courts of Medieval France.* New York: Harper & Row, 1972.

Carriere, Joseph. "Review of The Jack Tales." *Journal of American Folklore* 59 (1946): 74-77.

Chase, Richard. "Interview." Recorded at Berea College. Kentucky, Apr. 1975. Rpt. in *Southern Jack Tales.* Donald Davis. Little Rock: August House, 1992. 11-12.

—*The Jack Tales.* Massachusetts: Houghton Mifflin, 1943.

Coghlan, Ronan. *The Encyclopedia of Arthurian Legends.* Rockport: Element, 1991.

Crossley-Holland, Kevin. *The Norse Myths.* New York: Pantheon, 1980.

Davis, Donald. "Inside the Oral Medium." *National Storytelling Journal* 1 no. 3 (1984): 7.

Doddridge, Joseph. *Notes on the Settlement and Indian Wars, of the Western Parts of Virginia & Pennsylvania, From the Year 1763 Until the Year 1783 Inclusive, Together with a View of the State of Society and Manners of the First Settlers of the Western Country.* Wellsburgh: Gazette, 1824.

Donoghue, Denis. *Reading America: Essays on American Literature.* New York: Knopf, 1987.

Endoes, Richard, and Alfonas Ortez. *American Indian Myths and Legends.* New York: Pantheon, 1984.

Fielding, Henry. *Joseph Andrews.* New York: E.P. Dutton, 1946.

Finnegan, Ruth. *Oral Poetry: Its Nature, Significance, andSocial Context.* Cambridge: Cambridge UP, 1977.

Furrow, Melissa M. *Ten Fifteenth-Century Comic Poems.* New York: Garland, 1985.

Geertz, Clifford. *The Interpretation of Culture*s. New York: Basic, 1973.

Grimm, Joseph., and Wilhelm Grimm. "The Jew in the Thornbush." *The Complete Fairy Tales of the Brothers Grimm.* Trans. Jack Zipes. New York: Bantum, 1992. 398-402.

Hicks, Ray. "Jack and the Bean-Tree." *The Jack Tales: Stories by Ray Hicks.* Audio Cassette. New York: STS Music Group, 2000.

—"Whickety-Whack, Into My Sack." *Homespun: Tales From America's Favorite Storytellers.* Ed. Jimmy Neil Smith. New York: Crown, 1988. 10-13.

Hoffman, Daniel. *Form and Fable in American Fiction.* New York: Oxford UP, 1961.

Isbell, Robert. *The Last Chivaree: The Hicks Family of Beech Mountain.* Chapel Hill: University of North Carolina, 1996.

Kercheval, Samual. *A History of the Valley of Virginia.* 1883. Woodstock: Gateway, 1902.

King, James Roy. *Old Tales and New Truths: Charting the Bright-Shadow World*. New York: State University of New York: 1992.

Labov, William. "The Transformation of Experience in NarrativeSyntax." *Language in the Inner City: Studies in the Black English Vernacular*. Philadelphia: University of Pennsylvania, 1972. 354-396.

Lindahl, Carl. "Jack, My Father, and Uncle Ray." *Jack in Two Worlds*. Ed. William Bernard McCarthy. Chapel Hill: University of North Carolina, 1994. 27-33.

—"Jacks: The Name, the Tales, the American Traditions." *Jack in Two Worlds*. Ed. William Bernard McCarthy. Chapel Hill: University of North Carolina, 1994. xv-xxxiv.

Long, Maude Gentry. "Jack and the Heifer Hide." *Jack in Two Worlds*. Ed. William Bernard McCarthy. Chapel Hill: University of North Carolina, 1994. 107-122.

Lord, Albert B. *The Singer of Tales*. Cambridge: Harvard UP, 1960.

May, Jim. "Soldier Jack Meets the Purple Bogies." *Purple Bogies and Other Ghost Tales*. Audiocassette. Bell Farm Recordings, 1986.

—*The Farm on Nippersink Creek*. Little Rock: August House, 1994.

McDermitt, Barbara. "Storytelling and a Boy Named Jack." *North Carolina Folklore Journal* 31 (1983): 3-22.

Nicolaison, W.F.H. "The Teller and the Tale: Storytelling on Beech Mountain." *Jack in Two Worlds*. Ed. William Bernard McCarthy. Chapel Hill: University of North Carolina, 1994. 123-149.

Ong, Walter J. *Orality & Literacy: The Technologizing of the Word*. New York: Routledge, 1988.

Opie, Iona., and Peter Opie. *The Classic Fairy Tales*. New York: Oxford UP, 1974.

—*The Oxford Dictionary of Nursery Rhymes*. London: Oxford UP, 1973.

Parry, Milman. *The Making of Homeric Verse*. Ed. Adam Parry. New York: Oxford UP, 1971.

Polanyi, Livia. *Telling the American Story: A Structural and Cultural Analysis of Conversational Storytelling*. New Jersey: Ablex, 1985.

Proffitt, Jr., Frank. "Jack and the Old Rich Man." *Jack in Two Worlds*. Ed. William Bernard McCarthy. Chapel Hill: University of North Carolina, 1994. 34-55.

Propp, Vladimir. *Morphology of the Folktale*. Trans. Laurence Scott. Ed. Louis A. Wagner. Austin: University of Texas, 1998.

—*Theory and History of Folklore*. Trans. A.Y. Martin and R.P. Martin. Minneapolis: University of Minnesota, 1984.

Saussure, Ferdinand de. *Course in General Linguistics*. Tr. Wade Baskin. Eds. Charles Bally and Albert Sechehaye. New York: Philosophical Library, 1959.

Scholes, Robert., and Robert Kellogg. *The Nature of Narrative*. New York: Oxford UP, 1966.

Scholes, Robert. *Structuralism in Literature*. New Haven: Yale UP, 1974.

Shakespeare, William. "As You Like It." *The Riverside Shakespeare*. Ed. G. Blakemore Evans. Boston: Houghton Mifflin, 1974. 369-402.

Simms, Laura. "The Lamplighter: The Storyteller in the Modern World." *National Storytelling Journal* 1 no. 1 (1984): 8-11.

Smith, Jimmy Neil. "Ray Hicks." *Homespun: Tales From America's Favorite Storytellers*. Ed. Jimmy Neil Smith. New York: Crown, 1988. 4-9.

Sobol, Joseph Daniel. "Jack in the Raw: Ray Hicks." *Jack in Two Worlds*. Ed. William Bernard McCarthy. Chapel Hill: North Carolina UP, 1994. 3-9.

—"The Jack Tales: Coming From Afar." *Southern Jack Tales*. Donald Davis. Little Rock: August House, 1992. 11-23.

—*The Storyteller's Journey: An American Revival.* Chicago: University of Illinois, 1999.

Stivender, Ed. "Hardy Hard-Head." *A Storytelling Treasury: Tales Told at the 20th-Anniversary National Storytelling Festival.* Audio Cassette. Ed. Carol Birch. Jonesborough: National Storytelling, 1992.

—"Jack and the Robbers." *Homespun: Tales From America's Favorite Storytellers.* Ed. Jimmy Neil Smith. New York: Crown, 1988. 68-71.

Stone, Kay. "Jack's Adventures in Toronto." *Jack in Two Worlds.* Ed. William Bernard McCarthy. Chapel Hill: University of North Carolina, 1994. 250-256.

Tannen, Deborah. *Talking Voices: Repetition, Dialogue, and Imagery in Conversational Discourse.* New York: Cambridge UP, 1989.

Yolen, Jane. *Touch Magic: Fantasy, Faerie & Folklore in the Literature of Childhood.* Little Rock: August House, 2000.

Zipes, Jack. "Once There Were Two Brothers Named Grimm." *The Complete Fairy Tales of the Brothers Grimm.* Trans. Jack Zipes. New York: Bantum, 1992. xvii-xxxi.

About the Author

Christine Pavesic received her Ph.D. from Northern Illinois University where her studies focused on tracing the development of American oral literature. She is a long-standing member of both the Modern Language Association of America and the National Storytelling Network.

Dr. Pavesic has published many short stories, including "Sarah's Story," a Winner in the 1997 *Troubadours'* Short Story Contest. In 2003 she presented "The Jack Tales in Illinois: Continuing the Oral Tradition" at the Illinois Historic Preservation Agency's Conference on Illinois History.

She currently teaches English at both the University of Wisconsin and Upper Iowa University. In 2005, the students and administration at Upper Iowa presented her with the Excellence in Teaching Award.

Endnotes

1. After migrating to America, fablieux were absorbed in the oral tradition and emerged as naturalized Appalachian Jack Tales. For example, the title character of the fabliau "The Sacristan Monk," located in Paul Brians' *Bawdy Tales from the Courts of Medieval France*, can be found in Chase's version of "Old Dry Frye." Donald Davis' "The Time Jack Fooled the Miller" contains similar elements to Chaucer's "The Reeve's Tale."

2. This view of childhood only held true for the upper and middle classes. Most lower class Victorian children still labored long hours in the fields and factories—as Charles Dickens portrayed in his fiction.

3. The index follows the same format established by F.J. Child in *English and Scottish Popular Ballads*. Folktales which have surmounted the barriers of language, geography, and culture are referred to by numbers and types in the Aarne-Thompson index.

4. The legend of King Arthur and his Knights of Camelot is part of the traditional lore of Britain and arose during a time when cultural values were undergoing a rapid change. The question of whether King Arthur ever existed is not as relevant as the existence of the stories and ideas associated with the legend. The name of King Arthur was attached to the character of a British military leader in the fourth and fifth centuries A.D., during the period of late Celtic independence and early Anglo-Saxon invasion. The Celts came into Europe from Bavaria during the first millennium B.C. in two stages. The first stage, known as the Hallstatt culture, came in slow waves of people interested only in domesticating the European wilderness; the second stage of invasion, known as the La Tènes, began around five hundred B.C. and was military in force. In 50 B.C., under Caesar, the Romans invaded England and overlaid their society upon the Celtic warrior traditions. In A.D. 450, the Romans withdrew from England and left the Romanized Celts, now called Britons, at the mercy of the Anglo-Saxon invaders: These Germanic tribes forced most of the Britons out of England and into Wales and Scotland. This is the period of the war leader Arthur, a man who fought for the Britons against the

92   Ray Hicks and the Jack Tales

invaders. The chroniclers of the time, Gildas (d. 570) and Nennius (Fl. ca. 800), refer to Arthur as a <u>dux bellorum</u>, or a war leader. He was a native warrior trained by the Romans and assisted the native British kings in battle.

5. In several other legends, Thor is often referred to by the honorary title of "the giant killer." See *The Norse Myths*, edited by Kevin Crossley-Holland.

6. Two of the male names which occur more than five times in the collection of nursery rhymes are John (8) and Tom (12). In English, John is considered a formal form of the name Jack. In *The Classic Fairy Tales*, Opie and Opie relate the parallel nature of Tom Thumb's internationally famous adventure, *Tom Thumbe, His Life and Death* (1630), and *The History of Jack and the Giants*; Both tales include a giant who threatens to grind the hero's bones to make his bread. The stories are so similar in manner and form that one can speculate the names of Tom and Jack had been used interchangeably by the storyteller (38).

7. In *The Jack Tales*, Richard Chase presents two stories—"Jack in the Giant's Newground" and "Jack and the King's Girl"—that contain descriptions of a king's "farmhouse" kind of residence.

8. A buck dance is a loud and vicious form of a tap dance.

9. Strickland's variant has Jack "puttering about in the back garden" (Stone 253).

10. "Hello, what are you doing in that sack?" is the formulaic expression that Long, Ward, and Presnell have inherited. Each storyteller tends to place a different degree of emphasis on the opening greeting, but the basic interrogative sentence remains the same.

11. Proffitt Sr.'s version of "The Master Thief" is the only version printed word-for-word in *The Jack Tales*.

978-0-595-36377-3
0-595-36377-6